Palm Oil - Current Status and Updates

Edited by Viduranga Y. Waisundara

Published in London, United Kingdom

Palm Oil - Current Status and Updates
http://dx.doi.org/10.5772/intechopen.104286
Edited by Viduranga Y. Waisundara

Contributors
Eric Awere, Peter Appiah Obeng, Alessandra Bonoli, Sara Pennellini, Sara Bottausci, William Kwaasi Kwaasi Amanor, Emmanuel Kekeli Akuaku, Otuba Moses Amugoli, Gabriel Ddamulira, Alex Asiimwe, Fred Bwayo Masika, Rajasekhar Pinnamaneni, Kalidas Potineni, Ioana Stanciu, M. Chandra Surya Rao, B. Narsimha Rao, D. V. Swami, P. Ashok, B. Babu Rao, Viduranga Y. Waisundara, Kanchana Priyadarshani Samarasinghe

First published in London, United Kingdom, 2023 by IntechOpen
IntechOpen is the global imprint of INTECHOPEN LIMITED, registered in England and Wales, registration number: 11086078, 5 Princes Gate Court, London, SW7 2QJ, United Kingdom

British Library Cataloguing-in-Publication Data
A catalogue record for this book is available from the British Library

Additional hard and PDF copies can be obtained from orders@intechopen.com

Palm Oil - Current Status and Updates
Edited by Viduranga Y. Waisundara
p. cm.
Print ISBN 978-1-83768-065-8
Online ISBN 978-1-83768-066-5
eBook (PDF) ISBN 978-1-83768-067-2

Meet the editor

Dr. Viduranga Waisundara obtained her Ph.D. in Food and Science Technology from the Department of Chemistry, National University of Singapore, in 2010. She was a lecturer at Temasek Polytechnic, Singapore from July 2009 to March 2013. In April 2013, she relocated to her motherland of Sri Lanka and spearheaded the Functional Food Product Development Project at the National Institute of Fundamental Studies until 2016. She was a senior lecturer on a temporary basis at the Department of Food Technology, Faculty of Technology, Rajarata University of Sri Lanka. She is currently the deputy principal of the Australian College of Business and Technology – Kandy, Sri Lanka. She is also the current Global Harmonization Initiative (GHI) Ambassador to Sri Lanka.

Contents

Preface

The palm oil industry is one of the oldest and most prominent in the world and has garnered a lot of attention from scientists, manufacturers, businessmen, environmental activists, and consumers alike. There have been inventions, innovations, and new discoveries as well as controversies, debates, and conflicts associated with this industry.

Palm oil is popular because it offers superior yield at a lower production cost than other cooking oils. Thus, there is a noteworthy production of and demand for palm oil on the rise. It appears that palm oil plantations are rapidly spreading across Asia, Africa, and Latin America, although this comes at the expense of the depletion of tropical forests. Nevertheless, the palm oil industry being a sustainable and economically viable industry, discussions and implementations on remedying this situation are constantly ongoing. Regulatory frameworks are being developed and improved to make the palm oil industry more "green" and environmentally friendly.

This book examines the basics of the palm oil industry as well as the processes and procedures involved. It is organized into two sections that include chapters written by experts in the field. It is a useful resource that examines the palm oil industry from various perspectives, providing a holistic overview of the subject.

I would like to take this opportunity to extend my appreciation to the contributing authors for their excellent chapters. Also, my heartfelt appreciation goes to the staff at IntechOpen, especially Author Service Manager Ms. Blanka Gugic for her valuable assistance and support.

I hope this book will be one of many to be published about palm oil and the industry itself. It is important that the gaps and voids are recognized and duly addressed for the betterment of the industry as well as the livelihood of individuals who rely on it.

Dr. Viduranga Y. Waisundara
Deputy Principal,
Australian College of Business and Technology,
Kandy Campus,
Kandy, Sri Lanka

Section 1

The Basics of Palm Oil

Chapter 1

Introductory Chapter: An Overview of Palm Oil

Kanchana Samarasinghe and Viduranga Y. Waisundara

1. Introduction

This chapter is meant to summarize and introduce palm oil, its functions, comparisons and contrasts, and composition. Its purpose is to set the stage for readers who are new to the topic of palm oil so that the foundation will be set to go deeper into this mass industry—both technically and scientifically. Palm oil has become a valuable commodity and an essential aspect of many culinary and industrial applications. Thus, it is timely that innovations, technologies, and inventions are set to develop the palm oil industry to the next level—possibly in an eco-friendly manner while preserving its functional properties.

The genus Elaeis comes in two species: *Elaeis guineensis* and *Elaeis oleifera*. *E. oleifera*, sometimes known as American palm oil, is more environmentally adaptable than *E. guineensis*, which is known as African palm oil [1]. Compared with other regions of the world, Africa has a wider range of oil palm varieties in general. Palm oil contains a considerable percentage of saturated fatty acids such as stearic acids and palmitic acids; however, it does not contribute to arterial thrombosis or atherosclerosis due to the cardioprotective effect that is present in palm oil [2].

A tropical rainforest, with an average annual rainfall of 1780–2280 mm and temperatures ranging from 24 to 30°C, is the natural environment in which oil palms usually grow. The plum-shaped fruits grow in groups of 200–300 along pedicels near to the truck after the female flowers have completed their pollination process. The fruit consists of an oil-rich seed, which is also called the kernel. A typical palm fruit measures about 3.5 cm long and weighs approximately 3.5–4.0 grams. According to research, palm oil utilized in Chinese diets has a substantial ability to lower cholesterol levels when compared to other oils [3].

2. Functional properties and bioactive in palm oil

The predominant bioactive compounds and their health benefits are listed in **Table 1**. Palm oil is currently eaten as a dietary fat intake as part of a well-balanced diet around the world [3]. The use of palm oil for culinary purposes dates back thousands of years in the African and Asian continents [3].

There are several phospholipids present in palm oil that enhance brain functioning and nutrient absorption, which are shown in **Table 2**.

Ubiquinones and phytosterols are present in trace amounts in refined palm oil, often known as red palm oil (RPO). Furthermore, research has demonstrated that

Bioactive compounds	Health benefits	References
Tocopherols	Tocopherols reduce the likelihood of cancer, neurological disorders such as Parkinson's and Alzheimer's disease, and heart disease and boost immunity.	[4]
Carotenoids	Carotenoids protect against certain types of cancer by decreasing aberrant cell development and improving gap junctional communication. Carotenoids also aid in preventing heart disease by inhibiting the development and oxidation of LDL.	[5]
Phytosterols	Phytosterols can lower LDL cholesterol concentrations.	[6]
Tocotrienols	Tocotrienols can lower the influence of other cardiac risk factors, such as excessive cholesterol, on cardiovascular health. It can also prevent free radical damage and reverse inflammation.	[7]
Phenolic acids	Phenolic acids have anti-inflammatory properties.	[8]

Table 1.
Bioactive compounds present in palm oil and their potential health benefits.

Phospholipids	Functions
Phosphatidylcholine	Improves cognitive functioning, prevents fat formation in the liver, and regulates the body's energy metabolism [9].
Phosphatidylethanolamine	Regulates body energy metabolism and works as a chaperone.
Phosphatidylglycerol	Regulates enzymes [10]
Phosphatidylinositol	Phosphatidylinositol has the potential to increase reverse cholesterol transport by increasing cholesterol flow into high-density lipids [11]

Table 2.
Functions of phospholipids present in palm oil.

refined palm oil has long been recognized as a superior source of provitamin A carotenoids [12]. According to studies in red palm oil groups, retinol and beta-carotene levels were present at higher levels [13].

3. Processing of crude palm oil

Crude palm oil, which is acquired by pressing the fleshy fruit, and palm kernel oil, which is obtained by crushing the kernel that is in the middle of the fruit, are the two types of oil that are produced in general. A cross section of the palm oil fruit is shown in **Figure 1**.

According to research, crude palm oil requires several procedures to be refined prior to consumption in most cases, and this involves bleaching and deodorizing methods, which are basically used to refine edible palm oil in order to improve its smell, appearance, taste, and stability [14]. These procedures may change their original form in terms of color, odor, and stability. The differences between palm oil and crude palm kernel oil are shown in **Table 3**, whereas the differences in the fatty acid composition of palm oil and palm kernel oil are shown in **Table 4**.

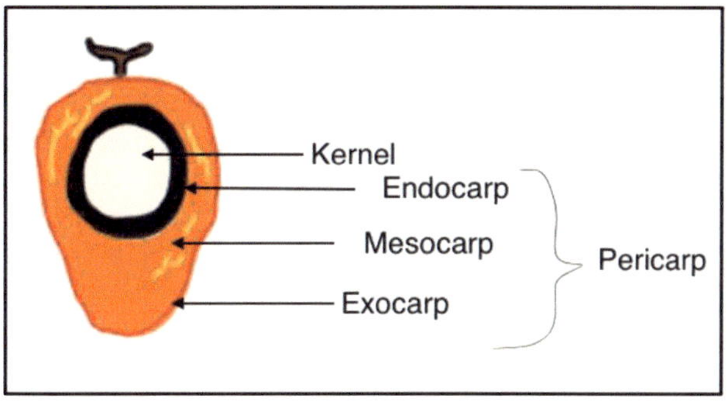

Figure 1.
Cross section of palm oil fruit.

Palm oil	Crude palm kernel oil
Basically used for culinary purposes when making food.	Generally used to make soap, cosmetics, and for nonedible purposes.
Oil is extracted from the outer part	Oil is extracted from the inner part
Balanced ratio of saturated and unsaturated fatty acids	Comparatively more saturated
Significantly low in lauric acid	Significantly high in lauric acid

Table 3.
Several differences between palm oil and crude palm kernel oil.

	Palm oil	Palm kernel oil
Caprylic acid (CL)	—	3.9
Lauric acid (L)	—	49.6
Capric acid (C)	—	4.0
Myristic acid (M)	—	16.0
Erucic acid (E)	—	—
Eicosenoic acid (I)	—	—
Oleic acid (Ol)	38.8	13.7
α-Linolenic acid (ALA)	0.3	—
Linoleic acid (La)	9.4	2.0
Arachidic acid (AA)	0.2	0.1
Palmitolcic acid (Pl)	0.1	—
Stearic acid (S)	4.7	2.4
Palmitic acid (P)	45.1	8.0

Table 4.
Fatty acid composition in palm oil and palm kernel oil.

4. Concluding remarks

As an industry, palm oil production has withstood the test of time and remains a valuable resource for many technical and culinary applications. There are many health benefits associated with the consumption of palm oil. At the same time, for many countries, the palm oil industry serves as a vital sector of their economies. As a highly studied area, it is hoped that the contents of this chapter have provided a general understanding of palm oil and the oil palm tree and thereby, demonstrated the necessity of studying further about this commodity and industry.

Author details

Kanchana Samarasinghe and Viduranga Y. Waisundara*
Australian College of Business and Technology – Kandy Campus, Kandy, Sri Lanka

*Address all correspondence to: viduranga@gmail.com

References

[1] Barcelos E, Rios SDA, Cunha RN, Lopes R, Motoike SY, Babiychuk E, et al. Oil palm natural diversity and the potential for yield improvement. Table 2. Frontiers in Plant Science. 2015;**6**:190

[2] Saleem A, Naureen I, Naeem M, Tasleem G, Ahmed H, Farooq U, et al. Effect of palm oil and their Main compounds in the Management of Cardiovascular Disease Risk Factors. Scholars Bulletin. 2022;**8**(2):59-65

[3] Odia OJ, Ofori S, Maduka O. Palm oil and the heart: A review. World Journal of Cardiology. 2015;**7**(3):144-149. DOI: 10.4330/wjc.v7.i3.144

[4] Kumar V, Rani A, Dixit AK, Bhatnagar D, Chauhan GS. Relative changes in tocopherols, isoflavones, total phenolic content, and antioxidative activity in soybean seeds at different reproductive stages. Journal of Agricultural and Food Chemistry. 2009;**57**(7):2705-2710

[5] Eggersdorfer M, Wyss A. Carotenoids in human nutrition and health. Archives of Biochemistry and Biophysics. 2018;**652**:18-26

[6] Trautwein EA, Demonty I. Phytosterols: Natural compounds with established and emerging health benefits. Oléagineux, Corps Gras, Lipides. 2007;**14**(5):259-266

[7] McIntyre BS, Briski KP, Gapor A, Sylvester PW. Antiproliferative and apoptotic effects of tocopherols and tocotrienols on preneoplastic and neoplastic mouse mammary epithelial cells (44544). Proceedings of the Society for Experimental Biology and Medicine. 2000;**224**(4):292-301

[8] Neo YP, Ariffin A, Tan CP, Tan YA. Determination of oil palm fruit phenolic compounds and their antioxidant activities using spectrophotometric methods. International Journal of Food Science & Technology. 2008;**43**(10):1832-1837

[9] van der Veen JN, Kennelly JP, Wan S, Vance JE, Vance DE, Jacobs RL. The critical role of phosphatidylcholine and phosphatidylethanolamine metabolism in health and disease. Bba - Biomembranes. 2017;**1859**(9):1558-1572. DOI: 10.1016/j.bbamem.2017.04.006

[10] Morita S-Y, Terada T. Enzymatic measurement of phosphatidylglycerol and cardiolipin in cultured cells and mitochondria. Scientific Reports. 2015;**5**:11737-11737. DOI: 10.1038/srep11737

[11] Burgess JW, Neville TA-M, Rouillard P, Harder Z, Beanlands DS, Sparks DL. Phosphatidylinositol increases hdl-c levels in humans. Journal of Lipid Research. 2005;**46**(2):350-355

[12] Dong S, Xia H, Wang F, Sun G. The effect of red palm oil on vitamin a deficiency: A meta-analysis of randomized controlled trials. Nutrients. 2017;**9**(12):1281. DOI: 10.3390/nu9121281

[13] Sivan YS. Impact of vitamin a supplementation through different dosages of red palm oil and retinol palmitate on preschool children. Journal of Tropical Pediatrics. 2002;**48**(1):24-28. DOI: 10.1093/tropej/48.1.24

[14] Rossi M, Gianazza M, Alamprese C, Stanga F. The effect of bleaching and physical refining on color and minor components of palm oil. Journal of the American Oil Chemists' Society. 2001;**78**(10):1051-1055. DOI: 10.1007/s11746-001-0387-8

Chapter 2

Evolution of the Rheological Behavior of Palm Oil

Ioana Stanciu

Abstract

Palm oil is dark yellow to red with a sweet taste and violet scent. Under the action of oxygen in the air, palm oil discolors due to the oxidation of carotene. The sample at different temperatures was recorded at different shear rates. Based on the rheograms (graph of the average shear stress versus shear rate), the studied ones proved to be Newtonian fluid. The shear range used did not significantly affect the absolute viscosities of the palm oil at different temperatures. The absolute viscosities of palm oil have decreased with increasing temperature and can be equipped with an Arrhenius-type relationship.

Keywords: rheology, palm oil, evolution

1. Introduction

The palm tree (Elaeis guineensis) is part of the palm family. The fruit has an ovoid shape and dark red to purple or even black. It consists of two distinct parts: the pulp from which palm oil is obtained (palm oil) and a hardwood shell, in which there is a white and oily core. From this is obtained palm kernel oil (palm oil), which differs from palm oil both in properties and in its chemical composition.

Palm oil is dark yellow to red, due to its high carotene content, with a sweet taste and violet smell. Under the action of oxygen in the air, palm oil discolors due to the oxidation of carotene.

The oil obtained from the core of the palm kernels is white to yellowish in color, with a characteristic smell and a slightly sweet taste. Palm oil is native to West Africa, where it has been extracted from the fruits of tropical palm (other than coconut) for over 5000 years. Until our century, this oil was produced on a small scale in African villages and only after

1920 became an important export product. Unrefined palm oil ("virgin" or red) is one of the richest natural sources of carotene, it is also rich in vitamins E and K, coenzyme Q10, and antioxidants. Although it has a high smoke point (230°C), palm oil is not recommended for frying, because after the first use the antioxidants are destroyed, and after four uses the carotene also disappears. It is used on an industrial scale as an ingredient for bakery and pastry products, for margarines and candies (especially potato).

Agricultural units are of different sizes and can be classified as small, medium, and large scale (estates). There are three varieties of palm trees: Dura, Pisifera, and

Tenera. Dura, the main variety, has been found in orchards for decades and was the main source of palm oil long before modern methods of cultivating palm oil were introduced to Africa in the second quarter of the twentieth century. Small fruits are without shell. Tenera also contains small fruits that peel easily to release palm kernels. Tenera palm kernels are smaller than Dura, although Tenera bunches are much larger than Dura bunches.

Palm oil is obtained from the fleshy part that surrounds the seeds, by crushing and pressing. The seeds are separated, and after being broken and peeled, they can be processed in turn, resulting in palm kernel oil, which represents about 10% of the total production of oil obtained from palm, the kernel oil is processed separately because the composition and uses are different.

Palm oil and its liquid fraction—olein, are used worldwide as cooking oil and margarine. Also, palm fats are incorporated into mixtures used for the manufacture of various foods as well as in the preparation of household products.

Originally from Africa, where there are still wild palm plantations and used for over 5000 years for food purposes, palm oil ranks third in world consumption of oils and fats, after animal fats and soybean oil.

It is generally accepted that palm oil originates in the rainforest region of the West African rainforest. The main belt passes through the southern latitudes of Cameroon, Ivory Coast, Ghana, Liberia, Nigeria, Sierra Leone, Togo, and the equatorial region of Angola and Congo. The processing of palm fruits into edible oil has been practiced in Africa for thousands of years, and the oil produced, very colorful and aromatic, is an essential ingredient in the traditional cuisine of West Africa.

In the fifteenth century, the tree was introduced to other parts of Africa, Southeast Asia, and Latin America. In Malaysia, the tree was introduced in 1870 as an ornamental plant, and the first commercial plantations appeared in 1917. In the 1960s, the production of plum oil was considerably expanded to reduce the economic dependence on rubber and coffee.

Today, Malaysia is the largest producer and exporter of palm oil in the world. In 1995, world production of palm oil was 15.3 million tons, of which Malaysia produced 7.8 million tons, or 51.6% of world production. In 2000, Malaysia produced 8.6 million tons of crude palm oil, of which over 8 million tons were exported.

Palm plantations occupy an area of over 2.5 million ha in Malaysia. The bunches are harvested manually and the transport is mechanized, and the processing of fruits and seeds is done in modern installations, of high technology and productivity.

Due to the high fat content of palm fruits and high productivity, the price of palm oil is usually below the price of soybean oil. Palm oil and its liquid fraction olein are used worldwide as cooking oil, shortening, and margarine. Palm fats are also incorporated into mixtures used in the manufacture of various foods as well as in the preparation of household products.

Palm oil is rich in carotenoids (pigments found in plants and animals), from which derives its deep red color and major component of semisolid.

Due to its economic importance as a high-yield source of edible and technical oils, palm oil is now grown in plantations in most countries with rich rainfall (minimum 1600 mm / year) in a tropical climate, 10° from the Equator.

The fruits consist of an outer skin (exocarp), the pulp (mesocarp), which contains palm oil in a fibrous matrix, a central part consisting of a shell (endocarp), and the core, which contains oil quite different from the oil palm, which resembles coconut oil.

This is equivalent to a yield of 5 tons of oil/ha/year (except for palm kernel oil), which far exceeds any other source of edible oil (**Table 1**).

Bunches/fruits	Composition
The weight of the bunches	23–27 kg
Fruits/Bunches	60–65%
Oil/Bunches	21–23%
Core/Bunches	5–7%
Mezocarp/Bunches	44–46%
Mesocarp/fruit	71–76%
Core/fruit	21–22
Shells/fruits	10–11

Table 1.
The composition of the bunches of palm fruits.

However, high yields are rarely achieved in practice due to unfavorable climatic conditions. Rainfall is irregular in Central Europe and West Africa and therefore the tree suffers from water problems. Expensive management of labor and production factors, imported fertilizers, pesticides, and harvesting equipment are also a difficulty that slows down plantation production.

The oil can be obtained from various types of plants. Large amounts of oil are obtained from the seeds, but also from the fleshy part of the fruit, as is the case with olive or palm oil. The most important crops of oil plants are in tropical and subtropical areas, and in temperate areas soybeans, flax, rapeseed, mustard, sunflower are grown.

Palm oil is native to Africa where there are still wild palm plantations, and the oil is obtained by simple, traditional methods. It has a long history of use for food purposes, with archeological evidence dating back to 5000 years ago. It is produced from the fruit of the palm tree called Elaeis Guinneis, native to West Guinea and ranks third in world consumption of oils and fats, after animal fats and soybean oil. The palm tree matures 3 years after planting and annually produces 10–12 bunches, each weighing 20–30 kg. A bunch can have 1000–3000 fruits the size of an elongated cherry that is made up of the fleshy part and white core kernels [1].

The approximate concentration of fatty acids (FAS) in palm oil is given in **Tables 2** and **3**.

There are many rheological models for interpreting data. For most fluids, the most widely used model is a three-parameter model, described by the Herschel-Bulkley equation [2–5]:

Acids found	Content
C16 palmitic acid (saturated)	44.3%
C18 stearic acid (saturated)	4.6%
Myristic acid C14 (saturated)	1%
C18 oleic acid (monounsaturated)	38.7%
C18 linoleic acid (polyunsaturated)	10.5%
Other fatty acids	0.9%

Table 2.
The fatty acid content of palm oil.

Acids found	Content
C12 lauric acid (saturated)	48.2%
Myristic acid C14 (saturated)	16.2%
C16 palmitic acid (saturated)	8.4%
Capric acid C10 (saturated)	3.4%
C8 caprylic acid (saturated)	3.3%
C18 stearic acid (saturated)	2.5%
C18 oleic acid (monounsaturated)	15.3%
C18 linoleic acid (polyunsaturated)	2.3%
Other fatty acids	0.4%

Table 3.
Fatty acid content of palm kernel oil.

$$\tau = \tau_0 + K\,(d\gamma/dt)^n \quad (1)$$

In this model, τ_0 represents the voltage or the effort of flow, signifying the minimum voltage that must be applied to initiate the flow. Obviously, being a voltage it is measured in Pascali (1 Pa = 1 N. m^{-2}). K is the consistency coefficient, the value of which depends on the nature and temperature of the fluid. It is measured in Pa. s^n, formally being a viscosity. The flow behavior index is the exponent of the shear rate, n. It is a dimensionless quantity, which depends on the nature of the fluid, its value being very little influenced by temperature.

The Herschel-Bulkley model is simplified and will take the form of the Ostwald model or the law of power:

$$\tau = K\,(d\gamma/dt)^n \quad (2)$$

Fluids for which the flow behavior index is unitary, as in Newtonian fluids, but there is flow effort (or tension) ($\tau_o > 0$), are called plastic fluids or Bingham plastic. For such a material, its behavior is like an elastic solid when the stress is below the value of the flow stress (or stress) τ_o. For voltages greater than the flow voltage, the mathematical expression for the model is [6–8]:

$$\tau = \tau_0 + \eta_p\,(d\gamma/dt) \quad (3)$$

This mathematical expression of the Bingham model derives from the Herschel-Bulkley equation when n = 1, and K = ηp. Given that the flow behavior index is unitary, the unit of measurement for the consistency index (K) is Pa, that is, the unit of measurement for viscosity. This is why K is replaced by ηp.

This article includes the study of the rheological behavior of palm oil at temperatures between 40 and 100°C and shear rates between 3 and 120 s^{-1} [9–12].

2. Material and methods

The rheological behavior of palm oil was determined using a Haake VT 550 Viscotester developing shear rates ranging between 3 and 120 s^{-1} and measuring

Physical and chemical properties	Stock
Melting point (°C)	34.2
Relative density (25°C)	0.8937
Refraction index (50°C)	1.455
Moisture and impurities (%)	0.1
Iodine index	53.3
Saponification index (mg KOH/g)	208.2
Hydroxide index (mg KOH/g)	22.9
Acidity index (mg KOH/g)	26

Table 4.
Physical and chemical properties of palm oil [8].

viscosities from 10^4 to 10^6 mPa.s when the HV_1 viscosity sensor is used. The accuracy of the temperature was 0.1°C. The physicochemical properties of palm oil are given in **Table 4**.

3. Results and discussion

Figures 1–7 show the rheograms of the palm oil. As can be seen in the rheograms, the shear stress increases with increasing shear rate and has a linear dependence.

In addition to the rheological models found in the literature, this article proposes two rheological models found on the basis of experimental data (**Tables 5** and **6**):

$$\tau = A + B\ (d\gamma/dt) \tag{4}$$

$$\tau = A + B\exp[(-d\gamma/dt)/C] \tag{5}$$

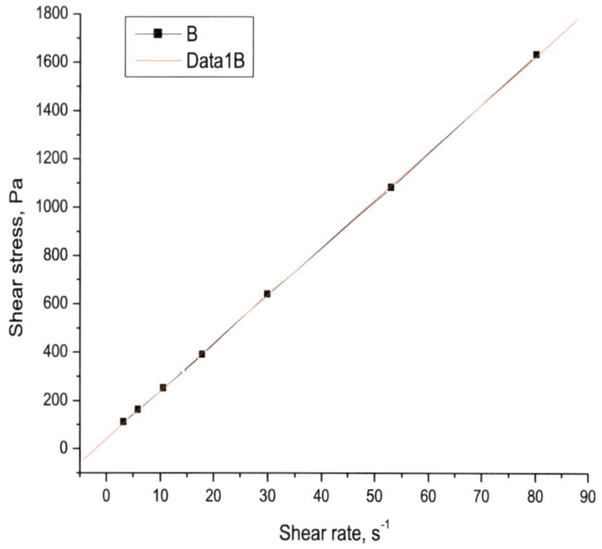

Figure 1.
Dependence shear stress versus shear rate for palm oil at temperature 40°C.

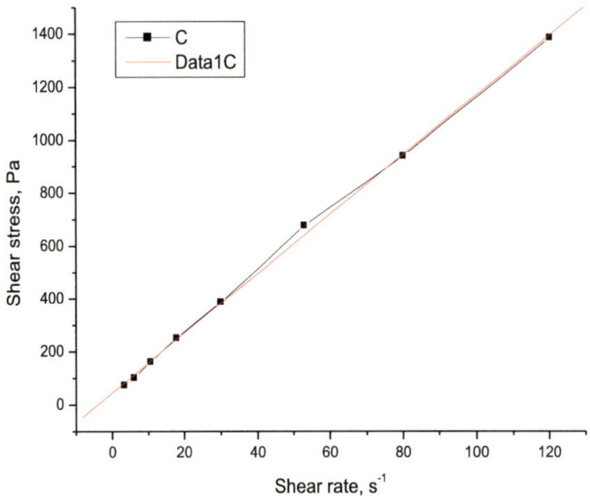

Figure 2.
Dependence shear stress versus shear rate for palm oil at temperature 50°C.

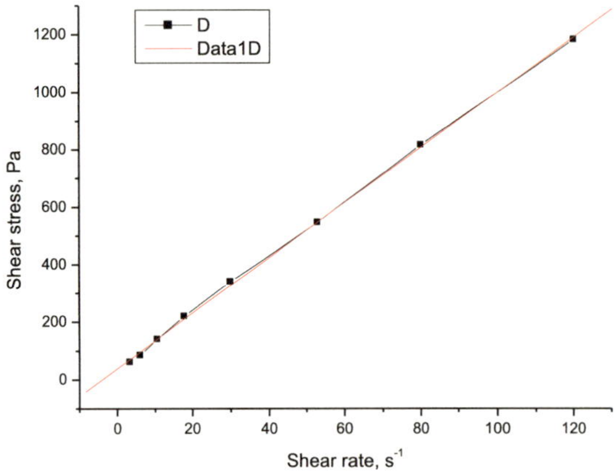

Figure 3.
Dependence shear stress versus shear rate for palm oil at temperature 60°C.

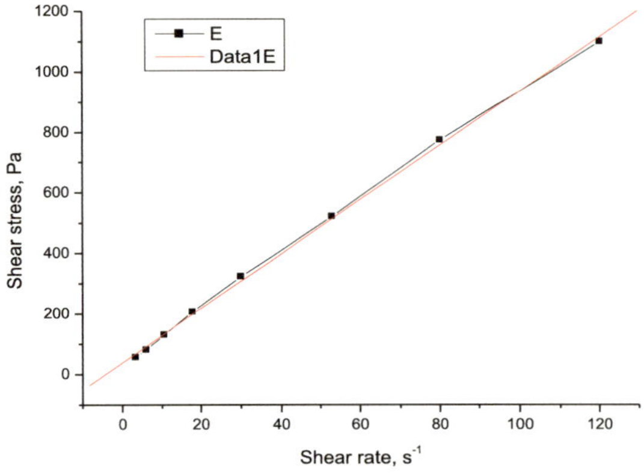

Figure 4.
Dependence shear stress versus shear rate for palm oil at temperature 70°C.

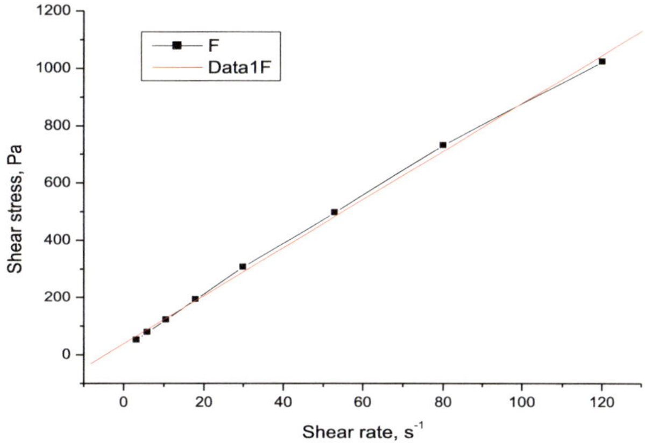

Figure 5.
Dependence shear stress versus shear rate for palm oil at temperature 80°C.

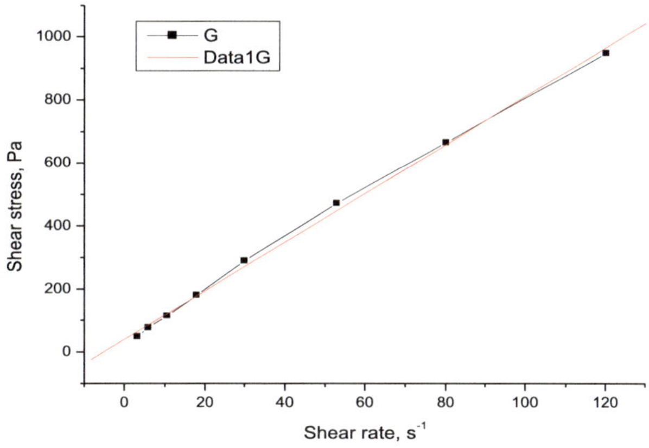

Figure 6.
Dependence shear stress versus shear rate for palm oil at temperature 90°C.

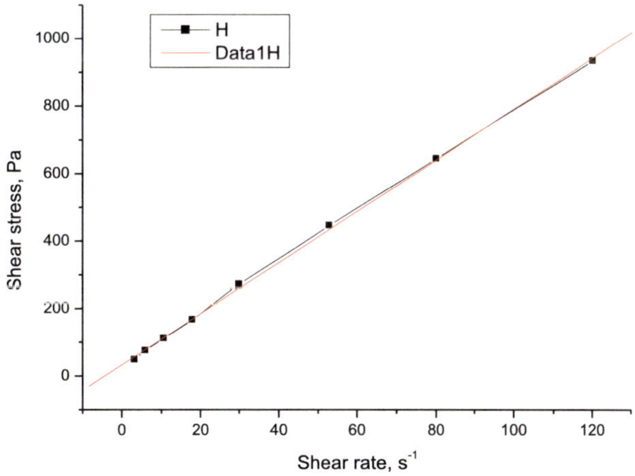

Figure 7.
Dependence shear stress versus shear rate for palm oil at temperature 100°C.

Temperature, ^{0}C	Value of parameters of the theoretical model described by Eq. (4)		R^2
	B	A	
40	40.8707	19.8184	0.9999
50	45.5434	11.2528	0.9995
60	38.8396	9.6028	0.9997
70	38.9844	8.9793	0.9994
80	38.2732	8.4015	0.9989
90	39.5068	7.7240	0.9989
100	33.0540	7.5880	0.9996

Table 5.
The temperature, value of parameters of the model described by Eq. (4), coefficient correlation for olive oil.

Temperature, ^{0}C	Value of parameters of the theoretical model described by Eq. (5)			R^2
	A	B	C	
40	−2.1256E7	2.1256E7	−1.0726E6	0.9999
50	8226.2569	−8194.2029	667.7298	0.9995
60	−9428.5756	−9428.5756	921.9126	0.9997
70	5055.5401	−5031.0308	499.1903	0.9998
80	3581.1580	−3561.7138	361.8749	0.9999
90	3159.7222	−3138.4422	344.0841	0.9998
100	5327.3930	−5303.8596	638.4288	0.9999

Table 6.
The temperature, value of parameters of the theoretical model described by Eq. (5), coefficient correlation for olive oil.

Applying model (4), the correlation coefficients have values between 0.9989 and 0.9999, which demonstrates that this model correctly describes the rheological behavior of unadditive palm oil used as a biodegradable agent.

Model (5) has the values of the correlation coefficients between 0.9995 and 0.9999, dedi, and it correctly describes the rheological behavior of palm oil. The two models were obtained by linear and exponential fitting of the experimental data.

4. Conclusions

The article proposes two rheological models obtained by linear and exponential fitting of unadditive palm oil. The range of shear rates at which the oil was studied is between 3.3 and 120 s^{-1} and temperatures between 40 and 100°C over the entire range of shear stresses. The rheological models found accurately describe the rheological behavior of palm oil.

Author details

Ioana Stanciu
Faculty of Chemistry, Department of Physical Chemistry, University of Bucharest, Bucharest, Romania

*Address all correspondence to: istanciu75@yahoo.com

References

[1] May CY, Nesaretnam K. Research advancements in palm oil nutrition. European Journal of Lipid Science and Technology. 2014;**116**(10):1301-1315

[2] Meijaard E, Brooks TM, Carlson KM, Slade EM, Garcia-Ulloa J, Gaveau DL, et al. The environmental impacts of palm oil in context. Nature Plants. 2020;**6**(12): 1418-1426

[3] Laurance WF, Koh LP, Butler R, Sodhi NS, Bradshaw CJ, Neidel JD, et al. Improving the performance of the roundtable on sustainable palm oil for nature conservation. Conservation Biology. 2010;**24**(2):377-381

[4] Kurnia JC, Jangam SV, Akhtar S, Sasmito AP, Mujumdar AS. Advances in biofuel production from oil palm and palm oil processing wastes: A review. Biofuel Research Journal. 2016;**3**(1):332

[5] Koh LP, Wilcove DS. Cashing in palm oil for conservation. Nature. 2007; **448**(7157):993-994

[6] Carter C, Finley W, Fry J, Jackson D, Willis L. Palm oil markets and future supply. European Journal of Lipid Science and Technology. 2007;**109**(4): 307-314

[7] Gibon V, De Greyt W, Kellens M. Palm oil refining. European Journal of Lipid Science and Technology. 2007; **109**(4):315-335

[8] http://www.medicina-familiei.ro/arhiva-articole/70-alimentefructe/

[9] Mukherjee S, Mitra A. Health effects of palm oil. Journal of Human Ecology. 2009;**26**(3):197-203

[10] Narváez PC, Rincon SM, Sanchez FJ. Kinetics of palm oil methanolysis. Journal of the American Oil Chemists' Society. 2007;**84**(10):971-977

[11] Maclellan M. Palm oil. Journal of the American Oil Chemists' Society. 1983; **60**(2):368-373

[12] Gatti RC, Liang J, Velichevskaya A, Zhou M. Sustainable palm oil may not be so sustainable. Science of the Total Environment. 2019;**652**:48-51

Section 2

Palm Oil Production

Chapter 3

Management and Processing of Palm Oil (*Elaeis guineensis* Jacq): The Crop for Future

M. Chandra Surya Rao, B. Narsimha Rao, D.V. Swami, P. Ashok, G. Roja Ramani and B. Babu Rao

Abstract

India is one of the largest producers and consumers of edible oils and fats in the world. It contributes to about 7–8% of the world's oilseeds and 6–7% of the global vegetable oils and is the fifth largest edible oil economy in the world. Even though India occupies a prominent position in the global oilseed production, its average yield for major oilseeds is 40–60% below the world average and has been growing at a slow pace. India is having rich agroecological diversity and is ideally suited for growing all major oil seed crops. It is reported that India excessively import edible oil such as palm oil from Malaysia and Indonesia and soybean oil from Argentina because the average yield of many of these oil seed crops is very low, compared to other crops like palm oil. This stressful situation is further aggravated by some traders who indulge in malpractices of adulteration of these oils with cheaper oils and synthetic colors for economic benefit. This chapter discusses the state-of-the-art of crop management and processing of palm oil, which is considered as the future crop.

Keywords: edible oils, oilseeds, palm oil and processing

1. Introduction

Being the fifth largest edible oil economy in the world, India contributes to about 7–8% of the world's oilseeds and about 6–7% of the global vegetable oils. Even after occupying a prominent position in the global oilseed production, India's average yield for major oilseeds is 40–60 percent below the world average and has been growing at a slow pace. The majority of edible oil imports of India are palm oil from Malaysia and Indonesia and soybean oil from Argentina because the average yield of many of these oil seed crops (ground nut, mustard or rape seed, sunflower, sesame, safflower, and niger) is very low, compared with other crops like Palm oil. It is the highest edible oil-yielding crop giving up to 5–6 tonnes of oil per hectare per year among the vegetable oil-giving crops under the good agricultural management practices [1]. Palm oil is well received by consumers, especially as a means of cooking due to its value benefits and price advantage. It is a good raw material for the production of cosmetics, pharmaceuticals, nutraceuticals, etc. In general, it can be said that palm oil is a source of health and nutrition improvement, value addition, recycling of environmentally friendly waste, a source of diversification, import substitution, creation, and sustainability.

Oil Palm – the most productive oil crop

2. Health and nutrition of palm oil

Carbohydrates, proteins, fats & lipids, minerals, vitamins, and water are the major nutrients required by the human being. Carbohydrates, proteins, and fats will be break-down into and utilized for different purposes. Fats or oil is an essential part of human nutrition, and performs several functions *viz.,* forms structural components of biological membranes and acts as an energy source, and derivates serve as vitamins and hormones, protecting from environment, and act as insulation. Lipids or fats are available from different sources. In Western Europe, it is dairy and animal fats; in India, its groundnut and mustard oil; in South Asia, coconut oil; in West Africa, palm oil. Palm oil is also a major source of dietary fat in India, Latin America, South-East Asia, China, Pakistan, and West Africa for the reason that palm oil is the most economic source of edible fat.

3. Edible oil imports and domestic consumption in India

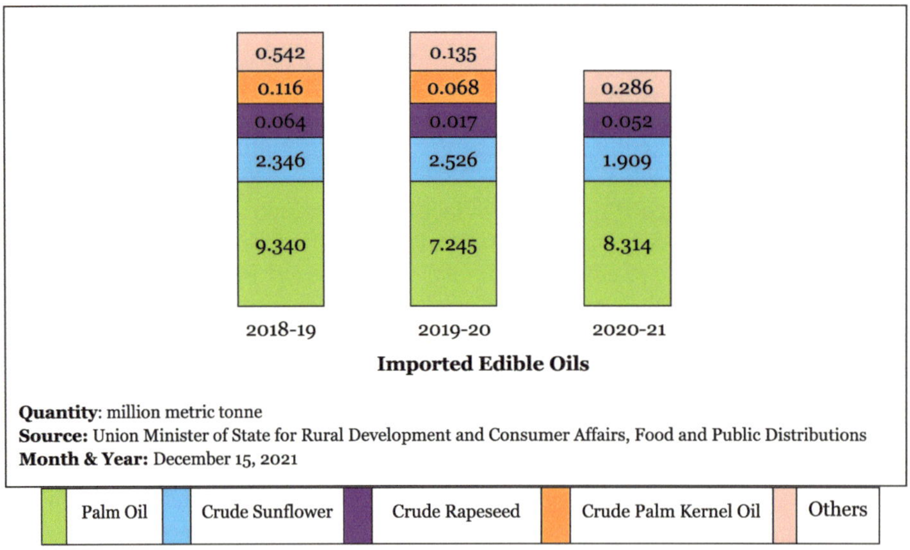

DOI: http://dx.doi.org/10.5772/intechopen.108579

Evidences state that palm oil inhibits the formation and reduction in the growth of tumors. Most important minor components of palm oil at a concentration less than 1000 ppm are alpha-carotene and beta-carotene (precursors of vitamin-A) and tocopherols and tocotrienols (precursors of vitamin E). Palm oil and its fractions are used in the production of margarine. Compared with unsaturated oils, palm oil is suitable for deep frying because of its relative stability to high temperatures.

Red palm oil is produced from crude palm oil by a novel process involving the pretreatment of crude palm oil followed by deacidification and deodorization using molecular distillation which is a carotene-rich refined edible palm oil. Refined red palm oil meets the standards of refined edible oil specifications and retains up to 80% of carotene and vitamin E. Red palm oil is the richest source of carotenoids, which stops free radical-mediated reactions. Carotenoids are known for their health-promoting properties that act as a source of pro-vitamin A and anticancer agent, and prevent cardiovascular diseases.

Tocopherols and tocotrienols are simply called as vitamin E, the principal role of vitamin E in the body is it acts as an antioxidant that helps in maintaining cell membrane stability and is the most essential for neurological function. Tocopherols are commonly available in most vegetable oils and fats but tocotrienols are rarely present. The most encouraging part of palm oil is that it is the richest source of tocotrienols that plays a significant role in exhibiting anticancer properties and greater physiological efficiency in inhibiting the growth of human tumor cells than tocopherols.

4. Palm oil-growing states in India

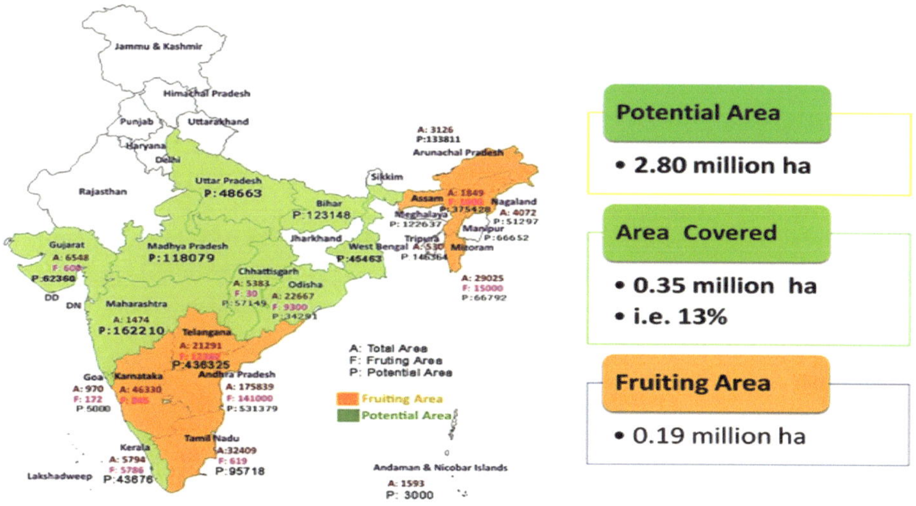

4.1 Botany of palm oil

Palm oil (*Elaeis guineensis* Jacq.) belonging to the family Arecaceae is considered as a smallholder's irrigated crop in India. It is a monoecious plant, belonging to Kingdom Plantae and Order Arecales. The term "*Elaeis*" was derived from the Greek word "Elalon" meaning oil, while "guineensis" is attached with its origin to Guinea Coast [2]. The other species of commercial importance identified under this genus are *Elaeis olifera* and *Elaeis odora*. *Elaeis olifera* is generally known as American palm oil. *E. guineensis* is native to West Africa occurring between Angola and Gambia, while American palm oil (*Elaeis olifera*) is native to tropical Central America and South America.

At present, palm oil exists in the wild, semi-wild, and cultivated forms, in three main areas of the equatorial tropical region. It is cultivated in 42 countries of the world and is largely used as edible cooking oil. The most important palm oil-growing countries include Indonesia, Malaysia, Thailand, Columbia, Nigeria, Papua New Guinea, Ecuador, *Cote d' Ivorie*, India, and Congo.

Portuguese introduced palm oil into Brazil and other tropical countries during the fifteenth century, while Dutch imported palm oil seeds from Africa and planted four seedlings at Buitenzorg (Bogor) Botanical Gardens in Java, Indonesia, during the year 1848. Commercial planting of palm oil was started in Malaysia from 1917 onward.

Indonesia ranks first in the Palm oil production with 32.60 million tonnes with a productivity of 3.57 tonnes of oil per hectare, whereas Malaysia ranks second with the production of about 18.93 million tonnes with a productivity of 3.83 tonnes of oil produced per hectare. In India, the total fresh fruit bunches (FFB) production and crude palm oil (CPO) are 12.82 lakh tones and 2.17 lakh tones respectively of which 11.44 lakh tonnes of FFB and 1.93 lakh tonnes of CPO are produced from Andhra Pradesh only (Department of Agriculture and Cooperation, Ministry of Agriculture & Farmers Welfare, Government of India, New Delhi, 2015–2016). India's share in the world's palm oil production is only 0.20%. At present, in India, palm oil is cultivated in an area of about 3.01 lakh hectares with an average productivity of 30–35 tonnes of FFB/ha/year.

Palm oil is a tropical plant that grows commonly in the hot and humid tropical climatic conditions with optimal temperatures ranging from 80–90° F. Henry [3] and Ferwerda [4] reported that an average daily temperature which is below 75°F is highly favorable for the cultivation of palm oil. Evenly distributed annual rainfall ranging from 2000 to 3000 mm is highly congenial for its growth and development. Zhu *et al.* [5] have reported that plants receiving direct sunlight of 5–7 hours per day have been found very much beneficial for optimal growth and development. Therefore, an adequate supply of water and the proper temperature has been identified as the most important factors in determining the yield of palm oil.

E. guineensis is a large pinnate leaved palm having a solitary columnar stem with short internodes. There are short spines on the leaf petiole and within the fruit bunch [6]. Palm oil is monoecious [7]—male and female inflorescences are produced separately on the same palm in cycles. The inflorescence is a compound spike or spadix carried on a stout peduncle and bears two large inflated bracts (spathes) that enclose the whole inflorescence. The inflorescences of both sexes are a compound spadix with 100–200 branches initially enclosed in a spathe or bract that splits 2 weeks prior to anthesis [8]. Palm oil is primarily pollinated by various insects [9] *viz.,* weevil (*Elaeidobius* spp.) in Africa and *Mystrops costaricensis* and *Elaeidobius* spp. in Latin America. The African pollinating species *Elaeidobius kamerunicus* was introduced from Africa into the palm oil-growing regions of Asia and the Pacific in the early 1980s. These introduced weevils have assisted a lot in the successful pollination of palm oil and significantly improved the fruit set thereby increasing the yield [10, 11].

Palm oil fruit is a sessile drupe and borne on a large, compact bunch, varying in shape from nearly spherical to ovoid or elongate, and is 2–5 cm long and weighs about 3–30 g. The fruit pulp, which provides palm oil, surrounds a nut, the shell of which encloses the palm kernel. The seeding radical grows at a rate of about 4.5 mm/day to a maximum length of about 50 cm [12]. Purvis [13] observed roots penetrating down to a depth of about 3.0 m in Nigeria, while Jordan and Rey [12] observed primary roots extending to a depth of about 6.0 m in the *Cote d' Ivorie*.

4.2 Ecophysiology of palm oil

Palm oil is traditionally grown in areas with an annual rainfall of more than 2000 mm and yields are always higher in countries such as Malaysia and Indonesia, which have more uniform rainfall compared with countries such as Nigeria, the Republic of Benin, and Ivory Coast which are noted for dry seasons. Irrigation tests conducted in these countries have shown positive responses to irrigation in terms of growth and yield. The availability of water in soils of palm oil plantations plays an important role in its proper growth [1] and serves as a signal for sex representation [14]. In areas where water is scarce, a large number of male flowers are observed to be produced, which is combined with slower growth rather than poor productivity. Basic information regarding water stress response in palm oil is a hot topic that needs to be further explored for controlling water tolerance. Water scarcity is a major biological stressor that spreads across the world over more than 1.2 billion hectares, especially in rainfed areas [15–17]. A dehydrated environment has been reported to be a major determinant of plant growth and development before the loss of productivity, especially crop species [18–20]. However, the basic knowledge of morphological, physiological, and biochemical responses in palm oil when exposed to water stress or deficit is still meager.

In India, palm oil was promoted as an irrigated crop, as the rainfall is much less than 2000 mm in most of the areas it is cultivated. It is estimated that about 150 mm of water per month is required by palm oil to meet its evaporation requirements. Under Indian conditions, several months of the year receive more or less rain, while the other few months receive heavy rainfall. A month that receives less than 150 mm of rainfall without sufficient water reserves in the soil is called a deficit month. When there is not enough water for evapotranspiration of palm oil, like other plants, this controls outflow loss by closing the stomata. When stomata are closed, photosynthetic activity is affected, affecting both growth and yield [21].

When evapotranspiration exceeds rainfall, the soil water content decreases and may reach a point at which the palm cannot extract water from the soil quickly enough for transpiration to continue at the potential rate. The palm will then start to suffer from water stress and the plant water potential will decrease. Under such situations, seasonal water deficit becomes the most important climatic factor affecting palm oil growth and yield.

A variety of different irrigation methods have been used for irrigating palm oil. The simplest and cheapest method is to control the water table level by flooding or blocking drains, but this is only applicable in relatively flat and low-lying areas. Other methods involve significant capital investment in the form of pumps and piping. Corley [22] suggested that drip irrigation might be less effective than sprinkler or flood irrigation. Plants subjected to water deficit not only show a general reduction in size but also exhibit characteristic modifications in their structure particularly the leaves with reduced cell division and leaf area. In such cases, stomata get closed early and gaseous exchange between plant and atmosphere stopped, and photosynthesis decreases earlier than the soil moisture potential reaches to permanent wilting point. Reduction in photosynthesis accompanied by increased respiration reduces assimilation in the plants and reduces the crop yield. Depending on the stage of crop growth, moisture stress has variable effects on physiological and biochemical processes.

In India, palm oil has been regarded as a smallholder's crop under irrigated conditions that have a marked deviation from the traditional areas, *viz.,* Malaysia, Indonesia, etc. where it is grown as a complete rainfed crop in larger nucleus estates. It is being grown in traditional areas with a well-distributed annual rainfall of over 2000 mm with no marked dry spells to areas of regular seasons with an accumulated water deficit of 600 mm per annum. The water deficit can be compensated by the provision of irrigation water. Also, palm oil requires a relative humidity of more than 45% for optimum transpiration. There will be a severe limitation of growth if the relative humidity is 30–35%. In addition to relative humidity, vapor pressure deficit also plays a vital role in influencing the growth rate, especially in the perennial crops.

Evapotranspiration is the sum of the evaporation and transpiration from plants. Transpiration is a continuous process caused by the evaporation of water from a palm leaf on one hand and its absorption by the roots into the soil on the other hand [23]. When evaporation exceeds the precipitation rate (rainfall or irrigation), a water deficit occurs. Groundwater deficit is the amount of water available from the soil in the active root zone of a crop. This is the actual amount of water needed to fill the root zone to bring the soil moisture level back to field capacity, which is the percentage of water remaining in the soil two or three days after the soil is saturated and the free drainage almost stops.

Water is an important component of plant tissues and a means of metabolism and metabolism in plants is essential for cell expansion by increasing its turgor pressure. In water deficiency, many physiological processes related to growth are affected and severe deficits can cause plant death. The effect of water deficit varies with the level and duration of water stress and the growth phase of palm oil. The leaf area can be reduced and this will reduce the amount of light that is intercepted. The reduced leaf water potential will close the stomata, so the plant will reduce its rate of transpiration, which is caused by an increase in leaf temperature, thus reducing biochemical processes. It will cause interference to separate the source and sink partitioning.

Even well-watered palms, as described by Corley [22], were found to close their stomata at noon when the sun was at its brightest and this could result in a 10% potential loss of yield. Despite high irrigation, low atmospheric pressures of relative humidity and high temperatures cause high vapor pressure (VPD) deficits, which can affect carbon accumulation. This was presented by Henson [24] who showed that the palm oil closed during the high VPD even though the soil moisture was not limited. Stomata begin to close when dehydrated, thereby affecting physiological processes [22]. Rees [25] showed that stomatal closure occurred during the second half of the day during the dry season under Nigerian conditions. Wormer and Ochs [26] reported that stomatal closure occurred during the dry season in Cote d'Ivorie. If the drought is prolonged, the palm can reach a critical threshold beyond which the water content of the tissue decreases rapidly. As a result, the leaflets get heated and dry out; hence, a large number of dried and broken leaves are observed as a result of severe stress. Finally, it entails the vegetative distribution lasting for several months or may cause the death of the palm.

4.3 Irrigation management in palm oil

Though palm oil is a typical humid tropical crop, it has been adapted to a wide range of climatic conditions ranging from tropical to semi-arid tropics. The climatic conditions prevailing in various palm oil-growing states of India are different from traditional palm oil-growing countries. In this context, irrigation management is one of the most critical aspects of palm oil cultivation. Irrigation is adopted to supplement the soil water reserve to meet the evapotranspiration demands of the crop, with an aim to increase plant growth and yield. A deficit or surplus of water would create stress on palm oil and adversely affect the yield of other crops. For palm oil irrigation without any deficit is considered optimum, which means that irrigation should be given at such rates and frequencies so that water is readily available for the plants with minimal losses.

4.4 Relationship between water deficits and yield in palm oil

Stage	Water deficit (mm/year)	Symptoms	Yield loss (%)
1	<200	Not a serious problem	0–10
2	200–300	Nonopening of immature and younger leaves, defective old leaves	10–20
3	300–400	Increased nonopening of younger leaves and defective leaves, drying of older leaves	20–30
4	400–500	Unopened immature leaves and dried leaflets	30–40
5	>500	Young leaves may not open, and leaf bud cracks and breaks	> 40

Irrigation trials conducted in different countries indicated that:

a. Yield response to irrigation increases with increasing levels of water deficit.

b. The increase in yield is due to an increase in the number of bunches with little or no effect on the bunch's weight.

c. The increase in the number of bunches is due to the change in the ratio between the sex ratio and the decrease in bunch abortion.

d. The effects of irrigation can only be seen after several months (28 months) after the irrigation started.

4.5 Palm oil-sensitive stages for irrigation

Two sensitive phases of drought in palm oil are sexual differentiation (approximately 30 months before harvest) and abortion (approximately 10 months before harvest). The second drought-sensitive phase may coincide with the photoperiod-sensitive phase, making their distinction difficult.

Moisture stress during the above two stages will result in more male flowers and the abscission of female flowers. Hence, yields get decreased. Irrigation at these stages can effectively mitigate the adverse effect on the production of bunches thereby palm oil yield. It is documented that the effect of soil moisture deficits reveals only 1.5 to 2 years later on palm oil bunch yield by increasing the production of male inflorescences compared to that of female flowers and by including abortion of female inflorescence.

4.6 Water requirements of palm oil

The water requirement of a crop is the amount of water needed by the crop over a period of time for its optimal growth under field conditions. It is a function of precipitation, soil water reserves, and evaporation. Water demand varies from place to place depending on weather conditions such as hours of sunlight, temperature, and wind speed.

Crop	Water requirement (lakh liters/ha/year)
Palm oil	67.35
Banana	120.00
Sugarcane	133.00
Rice	300.00

Water requirement of palm oil compared to other irrigated crops.

5. Methods of irrigation in palm oil

5.1 Methods to estimate water deficit in palm oil

Irrigation is adopted to supplement the soil water reserve to meet the evapotranspiration demands of the crop, with an aim to increase the growth and yield.

5.1.1 Rainfall-based estimation

The difference between rainfall and evaporation indicates the soil water deficit. To quantify the water stress, one should have potential evapotranspiration of the crop.

Water deficit for a period can be calculated by the given formula.

$$D = R + P - PE$$

where D is the water deficit factor, R is the theoretical reserve, P is the rainfall, and PE is the potential evaporation.

5.1.2 Crop factor-based estimation

It is the best available method to estimate crop water requirement from direct measurements of crop evaporation. Water requirements of crops are closely related to evaporation (evaporation of water from the soil surface) and transpiration (evaporation of water through leaves) when combined called evapotranspiration. Evaporation can be easily measured but transpiration is not. Therefore, it is much simpler to relate crop evapotranspiration to daily evaporation *via* crop factor. In this method, penman's estimate of evaporation is multiplied by the appropriate crop factor to estimate the potential evapotranspiration.

A crop factor can be defined as the percent of ground covered by the crop canopy, which varies according to the crop and stage of the crop. For palm oil, the internationally approved crop factor for an adult palm is 0.7.

The following simple method of calculation has been devised based on the evaporation rates prevailing in the area, especially during the summer months. For example, the highest average of pan evaporation during peak summer months is taken as 6.70 mm. The requirement of water per palm per day is estimated as follows:

Evaporation from open pan: 6.70 mm.

Crop factor: 0.7.

$$\text{Potential evapotranspiration (PE)} = \text{Pan evaporation} \times \text{Crop factor}$$

$$\text{PE} = 6.07 \times 0.7 = 4.69\ \text{mm / day}$$

As 1 mm of rainfall is equal to 1 L/m^2 = 46,900 l/day/ha.

Since 143 palm trees are planted on one hectare of land, the amount of water per palm tree per day is up to 328 liters.

Water storage capacity of not less than 70% of field capacity is acceptable and will not significantly affect the FFB yield of palm oil.

Therefore, the amount of water to be applied will be:

$$4.69\ \text{mm} \times 70\% = 3.283\ \text{mm / day or } 32.830\ \text{lit. / ha / day or } 230\ \text{lit. / palm / day}$$

5.2 Processing of palm oil

The first fruit bunches ripen 3–4 years after planting. Normally palm oil takes about 180 days from the time of emergence of the inflorescence to the maturation of palm oil fruit bunch. The majority of the oil formation in the fruits takes place during the last 2–3 weeks of fruit ripening. Harvesting of over-ripe fruits results in poor-quality oil with high FFA content. Palm oil fruits contain an enzyme called lipase, which splits the oil into undesirable free fatty acids leading to quality problems during storage, processing, and refining. Care must be taken to cause minimum damage to the fruit bunches and transportation of harvested fruit bunches to the processing unit with a minimum delay to reduce the activity of enzyme lipase.

5.3 Oil biosynthesis

Young fruits during the first two weeks of development contain very little lipids (5–10% per fresh weight). Storage of oil synthesis in palm oil mesocarp can be detected as early as 12 weeks after anthesis. A high rate of oil accumulation begins at 16 weeks and stops when the fruits ripen about 20 weeks after anthesis. Oil is stored in oil bodies found in the cytoplasm of mesocarp cells of ripe fruits. Small oil bodies may already be observed at about 13 weeks after flowering when oil synthesis begins. Oil accumulation in kernel begins about 12 weeks after flowering and stops at 14 weeks. During this time, the kernel gradually hardens [2]. The fatty acids in the mesocarp of young fruits consist mainly of polyunsaturated linolenic acid (18: 3) and linoleic acid (18: 2). When rapid oil accumulation begins the level of linolenic drops to an insignificant value, while the level of linoleic also drops but is stably maintained at 10% in ripe fruits.

Quartering is the process in which the fruit bunches are cut into smaller portions followed by stripping or loosening of the fruits from the bunch and spikelets.

Processing of palm oil fruits for edible oil has been practiced in many countries. Crude palm oil (CPO) is obtained from the fruit of the palm oil tree (*Elaeis guineensis*), which is a rich source of palmitic acid, β-carotene and vitamin E. Extraction of palm oil from fresh fruit bunches (FFB) involves field and factory operations. The techniques for processing palm oil fruit vary with available technology, and this will greatly influence the type and quality of the oil produced. The extraction of oils from freshly harvested fruit bunches involves five major operations: sterilization, fruit loosening, digestion, oil extraction, and clarification.

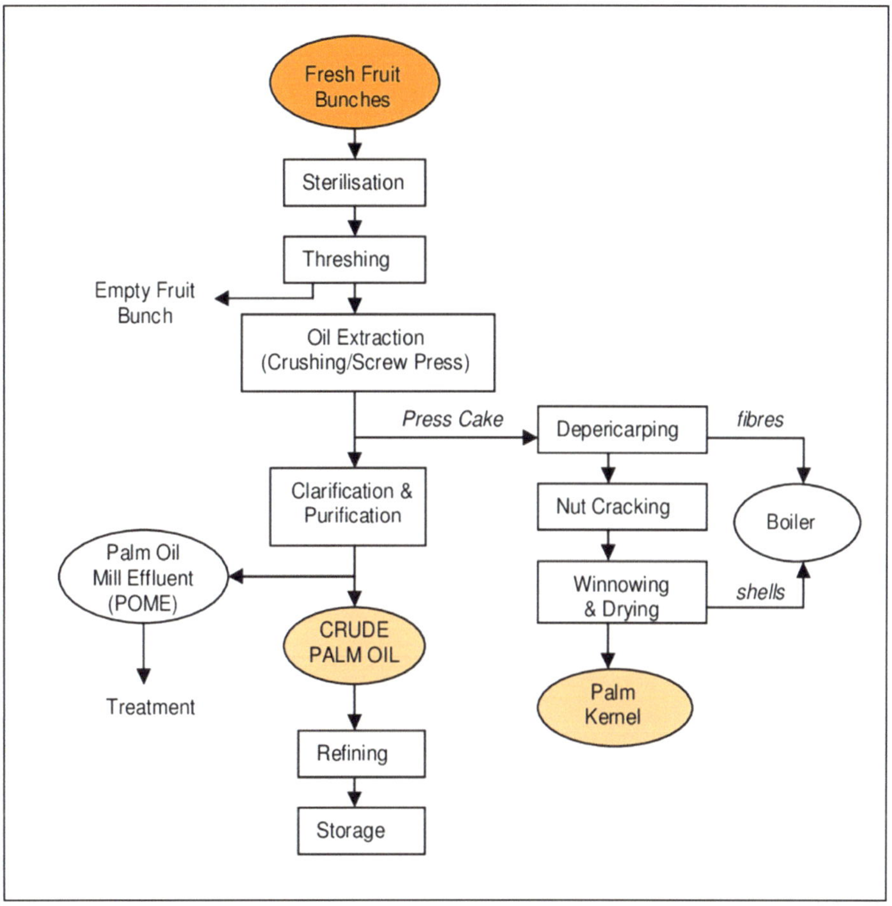

5.4 Sterilization of fruits

Sterilization or cooking is the process to use high-temperature wet heat treatment to loosen the fruits from the bunch. Stripping prevents free fatty acids build up in the oil and softens the fruits in the bunch to facilitate easy striping. The heat that is produced during sterilization destroys the lipase enzyme and arrests hydrolysis and autoxidation. Heat produced during sterilization will coagulate the nitrogenous and mucilaginous matters to prevent the formation 0f emulsions in the crude palm oil during the process of purification. It also helps in breaking up the oil-carrying cells of the mesocarp to release the oil during the digestion process.

5.5 Stripping or loosening of the fruits

Fruit stripping or loosening refers to the separation of fruits from the bunch and spikelets. Traditionally, it is performed by removing the fruits from the spikelets one by one even though it is a time-consuming process the fruits collected are clean and free from bruises. In the case of a mechanized system, rotary drum equipped with rotary beater bars detaches the fruits from the bunch leaving the spikelets on the stem. Stripping is carried out immediately after sterilization.

5.6 Fruit digestion

Fruit digestion means size reduction and it is a wet communication process involving the detachment of the steamed or heat-weakened mesocarp from fruit nuts. Digestion is to break up the pulp of the fruit and liberate oil from the cells. The extent of digestion of the fruit determines the degree of exposure of oil cells. Horizontal and vertical digesters are used for the process of digestion. Digesting the fruits at a high temperature helps to reduce the viscosity of the oil, destroys the outer fruit covering, and completes the disruption of the oil cells, which has already begun in the sterilization phase. The yield of oil greatly depends upon the method of digestion.

5.7 Separation or oil extraction

Oil separation is the process that separates the crude palm oil from the mash. In small-scale system, oil separation is achieved by combining digested screw press, hydraulic press, and hand spindle press, which are regarded as dry pressing (squeezing the oil out of a mixture of oil, moisture, fiber, and nuts by applying mechanical pressure on the digested mash). The other method is the wet method which uses hot water to leach out the oil.

5.8 Clarification and drying of oil

Last step is the processing of palm oil which separates the pure oil from the sludge in the boilers. Clarification is achieved by the separation of oil from water and other materials, the development of the characteristic product flavor, and purification of oil from contaminants. The oil from the clarification tank still contains 0.40–0.60% water and 0.10–0.20% of the sludge and other impurities that affect the quality of oil. The bulk of the water and the impurities are removed by centrifugation to bring down the moisture level. Further reduction of moisture to the optimum level of 0.1–0.15% is achieved by vacuum drying.

5.9 Refining

Refining of crude palm oil (CPO) is carried out for removing impurities, free fatty acids, color, and odor. This is achieved through 2 routes, chemical and physical refining.

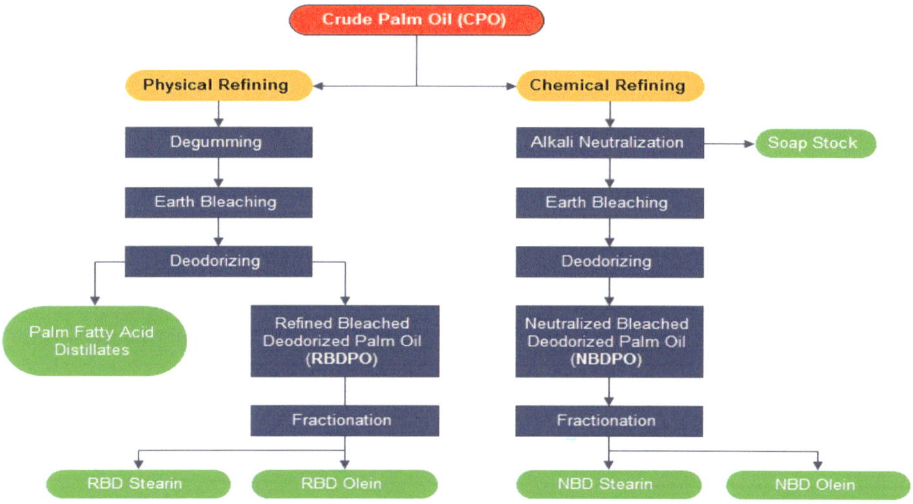

5.10 Chemical refining

Major unit operations involved are degumming, neutralization and soap stock preparation, bleaching and filterations, deodourisation, and polishing.

5.11 Degumming

The precipitation process in which the impurities such as phosphates, protein fragments, and mucilaginous substances are removed. Degummed oil is treated with a calculated amount of caustic soda to remove free fatty acids in the form of soap. The soap water was separated by centrifugation, and the neutral oil was washed out of the alkali and soap using hot water at a temperature of 90°C, then by vacuum drying.

5.12 Bleaching

It is done to obtain palm oil with a lighter color and to remove traces of soap. Depending upon the crude palm oil 1–3% of bleaching earth at a temperature ranging from 100 to 150°C under vacuum for 15–30 minutes is employed.

5.13 Deodourisation and polishing

It is achieved by passing superheated steam at 230–240°C under vacuum for 2 hours and the oil is cooled to 55°C and pumped through a polishing filter to give the oil its final sparkle.

5.14 Physical refining

Operations involved in physical refining are degumming, bleaching, filtration, steam stripping, deodourisation, and polishing. Crude palm oil is mixed with 0.21% phosphoric acid followed by bleaching with 1–2% earth under vacuum at 100–150°C and the spent earth is removed by filtration. The refined and bleached oil was deaerated and steamed under a vacuum at 240–2270°C. Finally, the oil is cooled and passed through a polishing filter. The physical method will yield better-quality oil and avoid contamination. The final product of both refining methods is the same *viz.*, refined and deodorized palm oil (RBDPO).

6. Conclusion

Palm oil is the highest edible oil-yielding crop among vegetable oils giving up to 4.0–5.0 tonnes/ha/year under good agricultural management practices [1]. Palm oil is well received by consumers, especially as a cooking utensil because of its cost-effectiveness. It is a good raw material used for the production of oleo chemicals used in cosmetics, medicine, nutrition, etc. In general, it can be said that palm oil is a source of health and nutrition improvement, value addition, recycling of environmentally friendly waste, diversified sources, import substitution, creation, and sustainability.

Author details

M. Chandra Surya Rao[1]*, B. Narsimha Rao[2], D.V. Swami[3], P. Ashok[3], G. Roja Ramani[4] and B. Babu Rao[3]

1 MS Swaminathan School of Agriculture, Centurion University of Technology and Management, Odisha, India

2 ICAR-Indian Institute of Palm oil Research, Pedavegi, Andhra Pradesh, India

3 Dr. Y.S.R. Horticultural University, Venkataramannagudem, Andhra Pradesh, India

4 Bidhan Chandra Krishi Viswavidyalaya, Nadia, West Bengal, India

*Address all correspondence to: suryahorti97@gmail.com

References

[1] Henson IE, Harun MH. The influence of climatic conditions on gas and energy exchanges above a young palm oil stand in North Kedah, Malaysia. Journal of Palm oil Research. 2005;**17**:73-91

[2] Hartley CWS. The Palm Oil. Third ed. England, Longman: Harlow; 1988

[3] Henry P. Croissance et development chez *Elacis guineensis* Jacq. de la germination a la premiere floraison. Revigen General Botany. 1958;**66**:5-34

[4] Ferwerda JD. Palm Oil in Ecophysiology of Tropical Crops. London: Academic Press; 1977. pp. 351-388

[5] Zhu XC, Sun ZM, Tao YQ, Gao WH, Huang QA, Cang ZW, et al. Introduction of prior variety of *Elaeis guineensis* from Malaysia. Guangdong Forest Science Technology. 2008;**24**(84):86

[6] Anonymous. Notes on the botany of the palm oil. Palm oil Research. 1962;**3**:350-352

[7] Beirnaert A. Introduction a` la biologie florale du palmier a` huile (*Elaeis guineensis* Jacq.). Congo Belge, Seventh Science. 1935;**5**:3-42

[8] Thomas RL, Chan KW, Ng SC. Phyllotaxis in the palm oil: Arrangement of male/female spikelets on the inflorescence stalk. Annals of Botany. 1970;**34**:93-105

[9] Syed RA. Insect pollination of palm oil: Feasibility of introducing Eledobius spp into Malaysia. In: The Palm oil on Agriculture in the Eighties. Incorporated Society of Planters; 1982. pp. 263-290

[10] Corrado F. Conformation of palm oil bunches colunbian plantation. Oleagineux. 1985;**40**:173-187

[11] Syed RA. Los insectos polizadores de la palm African palma (Bogota). 1984;**5**(3):19-87

[12] Jourdan C, Rey H. Architecture and development of the palm oil (*Elaeis guineensis* Jacq.) root system. Plant and Soil. 1997;**189**:33-48

[13] Purvis C. The color of palm oil fruits. Africa Institute Palm oil Research. 1957;**2**:142-147

[14] Jones LH. The effect of leaf pruning and other stresses on sex determination in the palm oil and their representation by a computer simulation. Journal of Theoretical Biology. 1997;**187**:241-260

[15] Chaves MM, Oliveira MM. Mechanisms underlying plant resilience to water deficits: Prospects for water saving agriculture. Journal of Experimental Botany. 2004;**55**:2365-2384

[16] Kijne JW. Abiotic stress and water scarcity: Identifying and resolving conflicts from plant level to global level. Field Crops Research. 2006;**97**:3-18

[17] Passioura J. The drought environment: Physical, biological and agricultural perspectives. Journal of Experimental Botany. 2007;**58**:113-117

[18] Blum A. Drought resistance, water use efficiency and yield potential – are they compatible, dissonant or mutually exclusive. Australian Journal of Agricultural Research. 2005;**56**:1159-1168

[19] Neumann PM. Cropping mechanisms for crop plants in drought prone environments. Annals of Botany. 2008;**101**:901-907

[20] Reddy AR, Chaitanya KV, Vivekanandan M. Drought-induced

responses of photosynthesis and antioxidant metabolism in higher plants. Journal of Plant Physiology. 2004;**161**(1189):1202

[21] Narsimha Rao B, Suresh K, Behra SK, Ramachandrudu K, Manorama K. TechnicalBulletin-IrrigationManagement in Palm Oil. 2016

[22] Corley RHV. Midday closure of stomata in palm oil in Malaysia. MARDI Research Bulletin. 1973;**1**(2):1-4

[23] Kramer PJ. Water Relations of Plants. New York: Academic Press; 1983

[24] Henson IE. Photosynthesis and source-sink relationships in palm oil (*Elaeis guineensis*). – Transactions of the Malaysian society of. Plant Physiology. 1990;**1**:165-171

[25] Rees AR. Midday closure of stomata in the palm oil *Elaeis guineensis* Jacq. Journal of Experimental Botany. 1961;**12**:129-146

[26] Wormer TM, Ochs R. Humidite` du sol, ouverture des stomates et transpiration du palmier a` huile et de l' arachide. Oleagineux. 1959;**44**:571-580

Chapter 4

Challenges and Opportunities of Oil Palm Production in Uganda

Otuba Moses Amugoli, Fred Bwayo Masika, Alex Asiimwe and Gabriel Ddamulira

Abstract

Oil palm, a lucrative vegetable oil crop in the world, showed promising adaptability to some agroecologies in Uganda from studies carried out in the 1970s resulting in first commercial establishment in 2005 in Bugala Island, Kalangala district. Further, adaptability studies continue to reveal suitable areas for commercial oil palm production in the country. The infant industry faces an array of challenges, both biotic and abiotic especially in regard to smallholder farmer field management and build-up of pests and disease in the face of climate change both in the nuclear estate and smallholder farmers' fields. The rapid build-up of devastating diseases such as *Fusarium wilt* of oil palm and Ganoderma trunk rot in Uganda is an interesting scenario since they are often expected from second-phase plantings in other areas in the world. However, it may be attributed to the all-year-round weather suitability to pests and disease build-up on native or alternative hosts in most agroecologies in Uganda. This difference from other oil palm producing regions in the world has resulted in recently initiated oil palm Research in Uganda to focus on developing local solutions to challenges facing oil palm farmers in the country.

Keywords: oil palm, Uganda, history, opportunities, challenges, prospects

1. Introduction

The Oil palm (*Elaeis guineensis* Jacq), most suited to areas between 10°N and 10°S of the equator, is a monocotyledonous perennial tree belonging to the family Palmae, Subfamily *Cocoideae*, and genus *Elaeis* [1]. The genus has two main species containing 32 chromosomes; *E. guineensis* the West African oil palm which is the commercial type and *Elaeis oleifera* the South American oil palm used mainly for breeding purposes because it contains more liquid oil and has high resistance to diseases [2–4]. Oil palm originates from West Africa, in the Niger delta, particularly in the belt between Guinea and North Angola in West and Central Africa [5]. It spread widely in the Palm belt of Africa through Sierra Leone, Liberia, the Ivory Coast, Ghana, Togo, Benin, Nigeria, Cameroon, and the Democratic Republic of Congo (formerly Zaire). Through large-scale commercial and small-scale household plantings, oil palm has now been introduced to countries like Burundi, Equatorial Guinea, Ethiopia, Gabon, Gambia, Liberia, Madagascar, Mozambique, Sao tome and Principe, Tanzania, and

Uganda where environment and climatic conditions are suitable. Globally, oil palm production has spread to South-East Asia, particularly Malaysia and Indonesia, which are now the world's leading producers of palm oil and palm kernel oil [6].

Oil palm is the leading source of vegetable oil in the world compared to other oil seeds with an annual production of over 50 million tons accounting for 39% of global annual vegetable oil production [7, 8]. Asia is the highest producer with 86.8% followed by Africa with 6.5%, Americas with 5.5%, and Oceania with 1.2% [7, 9]. In Africa, oil palm is/has been identified to be grown in over 25 countries and is mainly supported by corporate investors [10]. The area under oil palm varies from naturally existing stands in traditional plantations to large commercial plantations in most parts of Africa. Nigeria has the highest area under natural oil palm stands/traditional plantations with 2,500,000 hectares followed by the Democratic Republic of Congo with 1,000,000, Guinea with 2,000,000 hectares, and Togo with 600,000 hectares [3, 10]. In Uganda, one of the countries without traditional oil palm stands, commercial oil palm cultivation was introduced in 1998 through a Vegetable Oil Development Project spearheaded by the government in an innovative public-private-producer-partnership (4P) involving an integrated processor/nucleus estate/smallholder model in the district of Kalangala [9, 11]. Currently, oil palm production in Kalangala exceeds 11,000 hectares and the production has been expanded to the districts of Buvuma and Mayuge. Adaptability studies have revealed that production is suitable in Masaka, Kibaale, Bugiri, and Kagadi [11, 12]. In Kalangala, over 6500 hectares belong to the private sector partner, Oil Palm Uganda Limited (OPUL) while over 5000 hectares belong to medium and small-scale farmers. With oil palm offering four times higher yields of oil per hectare compared to other oil crops, yields of 6–12 tons/ha realized in Kalangala have helped reduce the oil deficit in the country. Furthermore, it has helped to reduce the high poverty rates that existed before the introduction of commercial oil palm production in the then fishing district [13]. Currently, over 5000 people in Kalangala receive regular and reliable monthly payments from fresh fruit bunch sales resulting in reduced fishing activity on Lake Victoria and effectively reduced Uganda's dependency on oil imports [13]. However, average yields of 8 tons/ha are relatively low especially in smallholder farmer fields due to poor agronomic practices, biotic and abiotic stresses directly affecting production. These challenges have been majorly unabated by the low knowledge base on the novel crop and the use of oil palm varieties from Asia, which are poorly adapted to local conditions in the first round of plantings in Kalangala. For example, globally, *Fusarium wilt* of oil palm and Ganoderma trunk rot are expected to appear from second set plantings where they have been reported [14] as opposed to the outbreak of the two diseases in less than 12 years of the first plantings in Uganda [15].

The major challenges threatening production of oil palm range from outbreaks of Blast in the nurseries, Oil Palm Weevil (*Rhynchophorus ferrugineus* Olivier), Fusarium wilt of oil palm and Ganoderma trunk rot, uneven ripening among others in the main fields.

Despite these challenges, the government through its National Oil Palm Project, NOPP has supported the oil palm industry through expansion to newly suitable areas and research for the identification of locally applicable technologies. This has ensured steady growth of the oil palm industry in Uganda over the past 2 decades.

2. Importance of oil palm in diets and income

Oil palm is an economically and nutritionally important crop in all countries where it is cultivated and/or its products imported. It is the most consumed vegetable oil in many countries in Asia, Africa, Central, and South America accounting for 39% of the total global output of oilseeds, overtaking soybean oil as the leading vegetable oil [16, 17]. Oil Palm is grown for its fruits from which the major products are derived including palm and kernel oil, and palm-kernel cake as the by-product [18]. Economically, palm oil products serve as a source of foreign exchange and as a raw material for industrial use. These oils are processed into a wide range of products for industrial and home or food uses where, refined, bleached, and deodorized (RBD) olein is used mainly for making cooking and frying oils, while RBD palm oil (unfractionated palm oil) is used for producing margarine, shortening, vegetable ghee, frying fats, and in the production of ice cream where milk fats are replaced by a combination of palm oil and palm kernel oil. Other than food uses, palm and kernel oils are used in industries to make soap, detergents, and cosmetics; in the chemical industry for plasticizers and coatings. The crude palm oil and its by-products including palm kernel cake, fruit chaff, mesocarp fiber, palm kernel shells, empty fruit bunches are burnt to provide electric energy and fuel (for biodiesel production). On the other hand, empty fruit bunches and palm oil mill effluents are used as farm plant nutrients and as feeds for livestock [18].

In Uganda, Oil palm is mainly grown for industrial use, domestically, it has reduced the country's dependency on imported oils and has provided a readily available source of vegetable oil for improving health standards and food intake. Financially, the production of palm oil has also improved the social standards of smallholder farmers and big population of people working in oil palm plantations for the nucleus estate. The others are employed by those with private oil palm farms and many others along the value chain get monthly remunerations from sale of ripe bunches [13]. Investments in oil palm production have led to improved infrastructure and service delivery in production and surrounding areas which have directly stimulated local economies and opened many areas to tourism around Lake Victoria. Nutritionally, palm oil is the richest source of dietary pro-vitamin A, vitamin E (30% tocopherols, 70% tocotrienols), vitamin K, carotenoids, and dietary magnesium.

Several studies have documented the special characteristics of palm oil. A comparative study with soya bean oil, peanut oil, and lard/fat reported that palm oil had an effect of reducing total blood cholesterol and "bad" low-density lipoprotein (HDL)-cholesterol and increases the amount of "good" high-density lipoprotein-cholesterol. Soya bean oil and peanut oil had no effect on the blood cholesterol but lard/fat increased the cholesterol levels [19, 20]. Other separate studies have also showed the benefits associated with consumption of palm oil in increasing "good" HDL-cholesterol in humans [21, 22]. According to USDA, a tablespoonful of palm oil contains 114 g of Calories, 14 g fat, 7 g saturated fat, 5 g monosaturated fat, 1.5 g polyunsaturated fat, and 11% Vitamin E. The wide range of natural palm oil fractions, have important nutritional and health properties, including antioxidant activities, cholesterol lowering, anti-cancer effects, and protection against atherosclerosis attributed largely to its tocotrienol content. Pro-vitamin E is vital for good vision, a healthy immune system, and cell growth, The major component of its glycerides is the saturated fatty acid palmitic; It has a balanced fatty acid composition of saturated and unsaturated fatty acids where the amount of the unhealthy trans-fatty acids is low in palm oil and it does not require partial hydrogenation ("hardening") to obtain solid fat unlike in some other oils and fats. Palm oil is the only oil with such good culinary characteristics that is cheap and readily available in sufficient amounts. Palm oil is the best alternative oil to use in order to avoid the trans-fatty acids in human diets [16].

As the World Health Organization (WHO) moves to ban trans-fats from peoples' diets, oil palm is gaining increased popularity and demand as a preferred safer oil.

3. Demand for oil palm and its bi-products

Corley [23] predicted that the global demand for palm oil would double and exceed 93 million metric tons by 2050. The increase in demand is attributed to general increase in global population, the relatively lower and stable prices of palm oil and the suitability of oil palm as a crop for vegetable oil production. Demand for palm oil is driven majorly by the food industry accounting for over 80% and the industrial uses including oleo chemical industry accounting for 20% [24]. Palm vegetable oil, a product of either oil palm fruit mesocarp or kennel, is widely gaining acceptance in the food industry due to the decreasing demand in genetically modified organisms (GMO) based oils among consumers and its associated health benefits. Oil palm can also be used in the paper and plywood industry, compressed wood industry, and the renewable energy/biodiesel industry [25–29]. Crude palm oil from the mesocarp fruit has been traditionally used for food in Africa for millennia and remains a main component of food, especially in the west and central Africa. In Uganda, the current entire oil-seed production meets half of the demand and the other half is mainly from crude palm oil imports from South East Asia. Both the locally produced and imported crude palm oil in Uganda are refined into vegetable oil or used in the manufacture of soaps and detergents. The wide gap in demand for palm oil for use in the food, energy, and manufacturing industries is an opportunity for Uganda to exploit through the expansion of oil palm production. This opportunity is being spearheaded by the government of Uganda and its partners through the expansion of oil palm production from Lake Victoria islands to other suitable areas across the country.

4. High income derived from increased demand for oil palm

In Uganda, palm oil and its products are mainly used as cooking oil and as a raw material for soap and detergents. Fresh fruit bunches from the nucleus estate, OPUL, and smallholder farmers are currently produced, gathered, and processed into crude palm oil at OPUL mills in Kalangala before being shipped for final product processing by BIDCO in Jinja. The production of oil palm and processing of palm oil is labor intensive and therefore generates opportunities along the value chain which contributes to an increase in different local income streams [30]. As noted earlier, Uganda imports vegetable oil yet there is an opportunity for increased production. The deficit provides an opportunity for local farmers to involve in oil palm production and alleviate rural poverty given the assured market for their farm produce through currently existing contract farming arrangements with large manufacturing companies. Direct investments in the oil palm-producing Islands have also led to the development of infrastructure and improved service delivery in these tourist hot spot areas generally boosting both the domestic and international tourism industry in the country. These developments as a result of oil palm production have thus provided wider avenues for tax collection by the government of Uganda from not only the different stages of the oil palm value chain but also other growing sectors of the local economy. Generally, Kalangala is performing positively on most development indicators, like roads, local income, farm roads, schools, health centers, and financial institutions contributing to the national gross domestic product (GDP).

5. Increase in demand can be met through research and development

Much as oil palm is still new in Uganda, some considerable amount of knowledge on the crop has been gained. This is courtesy of research with the research team based at the National Agricultural Research Organization (NARO). The research has from the time of inception focused on pests and diseases surveillance and integrated pest management system as a key control method, development of best agronomic management practices for optimal fertilizer uses, and enhancing the capacity of smallholders in agronomic practices to increase the yields [31]. Determination of optimal conditions for harvesting by determination of the time from pollination to ripeness maturity and maturity to fruit rotting. It should be noted that oil palm planting materials currently in use are being purchased from West Africa and South-East therefore, multi-locational trials, should be set up to identify the materials which are better adapted to the Ugandan conditions. Furthermore, training of researchers, in regional and international oil palm research centers both in Africa and South-East Asia like in oil palm breeding for training and acquisition of planting material for breeding trials are vital. Accurate and reliable data capture including weather data from potable automated weather stations and frequent monitoring is important in determining whether these plants can successfully grow under such environment [31]. Further, due to global warming, water retention techniques and some other cultural practices which lead to increased water retention and harvesting are important in oil palm production. There is need to develop an environmentally friendly method of breeding for superior oil palm planting materials suited for Uganda with good characteristics like disease resistance, oils with a higher level of unsaturated fats and drought tolerance with the help of molecular methods since the oil palm genome has been sequenced [32].

6. Challenges in oil palm productivity in Uganda

Despite only being in the second decade of production, the oil palm industry in Uganda faces several biotic and abiotic challenges which have limited production, productivity, and profitability. Production of oil palm started a few years basing on early basic agronomic research on adaptability and potential yields levels. Other production constraints such as fertilizer requirements, pests, diseases, and physiological factors were not prioritized at that time. Thus, the research information gap in Uganda is one of the main production constraints given the difference in environments. Some of the constraints observed in oil palm fields/plantations in Uganda are peculiar and do not tally with observed situations in other countries both in the nursery and in the field. In Bugala island, seedling take 18 months to mature and become ready for planting in the main fields and the time to fruiting has been found to be longer (we need to state the period here) than in other countries. Materials (varieties) grown in other countries have been found to respond differently in Uganda. These varieties have shown different yield attributes for size, number of bunches, un-even ripening, bunch rot all of which affect the production and productivity of oil palm [12].

Agronomic practices: Replenishing the soil with nutrients is vital for increased oil palm production just like any other crop. Oil palm is a heavy feeder and several tones of bunches are harvested and carried out of the field each year and hence mineral nutrients are removed from the soil. Therefore, fertilizers are an inevitable requirement and the major nutrient source in oil palm production. However, farmers do not regularly apply fertilizers in their fields and yet surveys show that oil palm plants have deficiencies characteristic of lack of mineral nutrients. Cover crops that would contribute to soil nutrients have not appealed to farmers and there is minimal adoption of both strategies probably because the fertilizers come at a cost and failure to maintain cover crops. Similarly, no nutrient studies have been carried out to determine the critical fertilizer requirements and the ideal application rates. The information gap and poor soil fertility management options hinder improved production and profitability.

Limited access to oil palm planting materials for evaluation: The oil palm industry in Uganda relies on materials from other countries which have breeding programs and are into seed production. The imported materials are intended for production without prior evaluation. Limited access to materials restrains evaluation and selection of the best materials for particular environments. There is a need to carry out a countrywide prospectus of the available oil palm germplasm and genotype and their characterization so that they can be a source of important genes when a breeding program is established since the oil palm genome has been sequenced [31]. This will also ease the selection of high-yielding varieties.

Physiological disorders: A number of physiological disorders such as non-uniform ripening, bunch rot, and bunch failure have been identified in Uganda [12]. Non-uniform ripening leads to poor fresh fruit bunch quality and high free fatty acid levels which affects oil palm profitability due to the rejection of pour quality fruits at the factory [33]. Bunch failure, the abortion of a bunch before it is fully ripe occurs between 2 and 4 months after anthesis [34]. It is caused by poor pollination and sometimes acute and severe shortage of assimilates caused by lack of water or radiation [14, 35].

Temperature: Temperature is an important factor in oil palm production. It can inhibit growth in seedlings by up to seven times at temperatures equal or lower than 17.5°C in seedlings less than 1 year [33]. Generally, there is undefined strong yield reduction at a minimum monthly average temperature of less than 18–19°C. Therefore, for good oil palm production, the minimum temperatures should be between 22 and 24°C and maximum temperatures between 29 and 33°C. However, there have been records of night temperatures going below 18°C on Kalangala islands which could be one of the key factors affecting optimum oil palm yield.

Pests: The major pest that constrains oil palm production in Uganda is the oil palm weevil, *Rhynchophorus phoenicis* [36]. At the nursery stage, chewing Lepidopteran larvae including the armyworm have been identified. In the field, the oil palm weevil has been recorded in areas where oil palm trials are established and across all the oil palm-producing blocks in Kalangala islands. The irreversible damage caused affects the optimum yield per unit area. The pest life cycle takes place in the oil palm host plant or other alternative hosts and during development, the larvae can excavate over 1 meter in length into the oil palm plant which dies within 3–4 months after infestation [37]. It is not always easy to detect weevil infestation before the damage caused by the larvae is seen. Measures taken to control the weevil have majorly been application of diluted insecticide directly on the affected and surrounding tissues. The efficacy of using pheromone traps and sugarcane as a lure are being evaluated by our research team but are yet to be adopted by the farmers. However, management of the weevil has been complicated by the fact that oil palm weevil larvae are a delicacy in some parts of the country like the Kalangala islands where some people rear them for consumption and sale.

Diseases: *Fusarium wilt* of oil palm (**Figure 1**) and Ganoderma trunk rot (**Figure 2**) are the major diseases affecting oil palm production in Uganda [15]. In other oil palm growing areas in the world, *Fusarium wilt* of oil palm and Ganoderma trunk rot often occur from the second phase of planting or following replacement of coconut plantations [14] as opposed to Uganda where they have been identified in the first plantings in less than two decades.

Other diseases observed in Uganda include; Blast disease in nurseries in Kalangala, and Leaf spot, Leaf rust, and Anthracnose in nurseries in Namulonge. Research in

Figure 1.
A Fusarium wilt *of oil palm-infested field in Kalangala district.*

Figure 2.
Standing (A) and fallen (B) Ganoderma trunk rot diseased palms observed at Kituza, Mukono district.

Uganda has adopted measures that include evaluating imported seedlings for resistance/tolerance to local disease strains such as *Fusarium wilt* of oil palm before being recommended to the private sector. Adoption of good cultural practices and selective use of tested chemicals are also being strongly recommended for use in the management of oil palm diseases in Uganda.

Rainfall: Generally, Uganda's weather is characterized by two rainfall seasons separated by short spells of drought around the Lake Victoria crescent where oil palm is most suitable and longer periods of drought in the North and Eastern parts of the country. Oil palm requires sufficient amounts of rainfall for efficient growth throughout the year. When all conditions are favorable, an oil palm plant transpires approximately 6 mm of water per day and this requires that there is a sufficient amount of water in the soil. However, the average transpiration rate in the dry season is 1.0–2.5 mm per day while in the wet season, average transpiration is 4.0–6.5 mm per day [38]. When the amount of rainfall is low leading to moderate or severe water stress, oil palm growth, and hence yield are strongly suppressed leading to delayed emergence of new leaves although old leaves do not wilt [39, 40]. Increased water stress, results in decreased photosynthetic rate and this is worsened by increased vapor pressure deficit even when the soil water is sufficient [41]. During the dry spell, oil palm production is limited however, research in Malaysia has shown that irrigation application during such periods produces a linear relationship between that water volume and oil palm yield [41]. It is therefore important to explore different options like irrigation as well other water retention methods.

Limited collaboration with other oil palm research institutes: limited research collaborations with other institutes or organizations involved in oil palm research especially internationally led to slow information and knowledge exchange. Similarly, technical backstopping is important for Uganda to establish a successful oil palm production value chain and research program. Poor information flow within the stakeholders hinders quick responses to production challenges in the nascent oil palm sector in the country.

7. Opportunities in oil palm production

The growing demand for palm oil is being driven by increasing population associated with increased demand for food with industrial palm oil products being central in the food industry and other associated industrial uses. Furthermore, in addition to the local market, the growing retinal and international market is pushing especially developing countries with suitable conditions for oil palm production including Uganda to adopt or expand production of the crop. In Uganda, this is being achieved through expansion of the area under oil palm cultivation through attraction of large commercial farmers and inclusion of local small-scale farmers in setting up new oil palm plantations across the country (**Figure 3**). Among other opportunities as discussed below, Uganda's equatorial climate characteristic of a mean annual rainfall of about 1180 mm and average temperature of 18–35°C with minimum regional variations in temperature and humidity favor growth of oil palm [42–44].

Breeding and biological technologies for oil palm improvement: Because Uganda imports most of its planting materials from other oil palm growing countries, there is little knowledge about the genetic quality of the planting materials available for farmers and research in Uganda. This has partly contributed to the poor physiological quality of the planted trials as farmers are unable to identify hybrids from

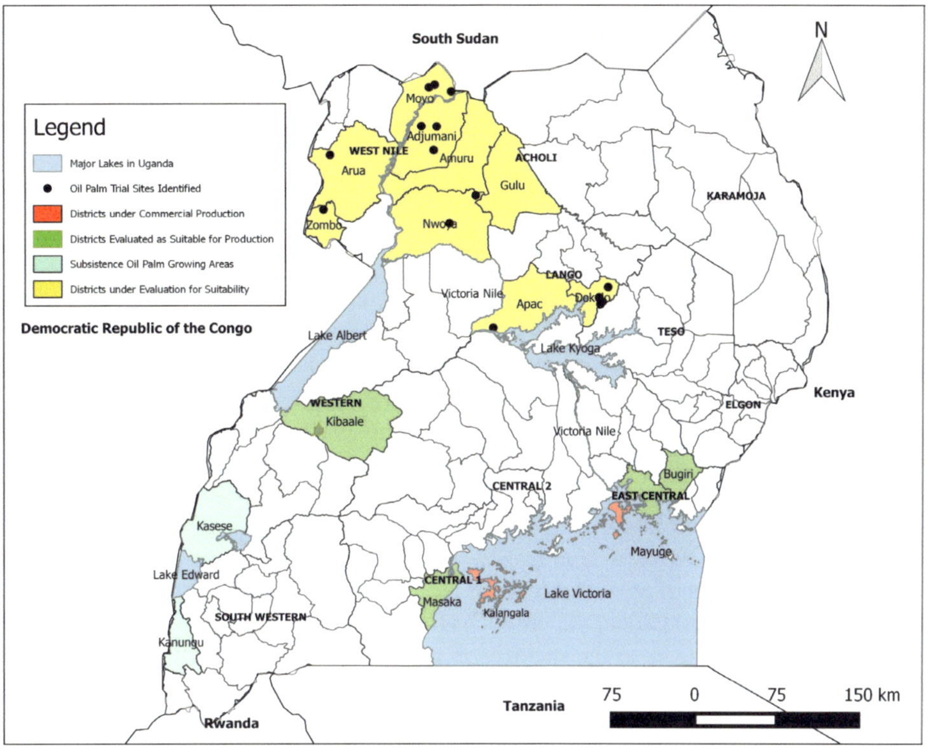

Figure 3.
Map of Uganda showing current oil palm commercial production districts and adaptability study areas.

non-hybrids. Therefore, in the long run, research in Uganda intends to identify and characterize the genetic quality of oil palm seedlings, using morphological and molecular tools. This will eventually lead to the identification of particular genes of interest to be incorporated in the breeding trials for the production of quality planting material that can benefit farmers while addressing local challenges.

Agronomic practices: Well-researched and precise agronomic practices (Improved technologies) reduce the costs of production and improve yields and ultimately profits. Oil palm responds well to good agronomic practices if it is grown in a favorable environment. The agronomic practices in the field start right from planting of the seedling through the management until fruiting. Some of the important practices that must be followed include fertilizer application, proper pruning, soil, weed, water, and nutrient management. Fertilizers take a large portion of the production costs under oil palm and must be applied judiciously to maximize profits. For fertilizer application, precise rates are applied to avoid wastage. Fertilizer requirements for oil palm depend on the resident nutrients in the soil that are basically determined by the parent rock and stage of soil formation. In Uganda, rates of between 1.5 and 2 kg of NPK every 3 months per tree depending on the age of palms are applied. Nutrient deficiencies from Mg and Boron are often identified, and in such incidences, rates of 1–1.5 kg and 60 g of Dolomite and Borate are applied, respectively, per tree. To supplement on soil nutrient retention, larger areas have adopted the use velvet bean (*Mucuna pruriens*) as cover crop. Further, oil palm factory effluent and empty bunches are being applied in oil palm fields to improve soil nutrient levels and soil characteristics. The use of velvet bean has been resisted by small scall farmers due to the high labor requirement to manage its vigorous growth, climbing attributes and the reported high incidence of snakes in such fields. For the above reasons, research has embarked on the characterization, multiplication and promotion of *Arachis pintoi* (Pinto nut) as a cover crop in place of velvet bean. Pintoi requires less management due to its short growing thick cover attributes which can make it easily appealing to farmers in Uganda and it is effective in controlling weeds, fixing nitrogen, protecting the soil from erosion and providing organic matter [45]. Weed management is also important in oil palm production. Weeds depress the performance of oil palm by depriving the palm trees of resources and suffocating them leading to few bunches formed per tree [46]. Manual slashing, chemicals and use of cover crops are the common practices used in controlling weeds under oil palm production in Uganda. Chemical use should be limited to a few times in a year because of the potential for environmental pollution, chemical residual accumulation and deterioration of soil and water health since production in Uganda mostly occurs around lake Vitoria crescent. Manual slashing is a bit costly compared to cover crop and efforts are underway to help farmers understand the value of this technology to reduce costs.

Pruning: Pruning is important in oil palm production and affects bunch production particularly the number and size of bunches. The ideal number of fronds per tree is between 32 and 40 with few fronds on a tree and un-pruned trees producing low yields [47]. The impact of agronomic technologies on oil palm production and productivity is obvious. It however varies with environment and location citing the need for tailoring such practices to the specific oil palm producing environments. However, in Uganda, knowledge of these management aspects is majorly applied basing on what has been done in other oil palm producing regions.

Tolerance to pests and disease: Oil palm is a perennial tree with capacity to sustain profitable output for over 25 years. This relatively long-life productivity exposes oil palm to gradual and/or rapid build-up of pests and diseases both in the nursery and the main fields. Oil palm is prone to infestation by various pests and diseases at different stages of growth respective of the growth location. In Uganda, several diseases and pests have been reported. Fusarium wilt of oil palm and Basal stem rot [15] are the major challenges facing oil palm in Uganda. These diseases have posed a threat to the oil palm commercial production currently at its infant stage. *Fusarium wilt* is the most important disease of oil palm in Africa and is notable in replanted fields [48]. In Uganda however, *Fusarium wilt* manifested in the first planting of commercial plantations in both young (<5 years) and older palms (>5 years). *Fusarium wilt* in older palms in Uganda exists in two forms, that is, "acute" and "chronic" wilt. In chronic wilt, the oil palm older fronds wilt before desiccating and breaking near or at some distance from the petiole and hang downwards around the palm trunk. The young fronds remain erect but gradually get small and chlorotic in appearance. In the acute form, the fronds maintain their erect position but die rapidly within 2–6 month. Internally, brownish-gray or black discoloration develops in the vascular system across the trunk as a result of build-up of plant defenses such as gum, tylose, and gels against the growing pathogen [48–50].

Basal stem rot is a disease of both young and old palms that restricts water movement within the plant causing failure of newly and fully elongated formed leaves/ spears to open, collapse of lower and older leaves from the petiole cloaking the palm trunk, drooping and yellowing of young leaves which later die back from the tip [51, 52]. Internally, both the roots and the stem are affected. The tissue in the lower stem characteristically turns yellowish from the inside and can easily break while outer tissue blackens accompanied with appearance of distinctive fructifications and often gum exudates. This is followed by collapse of the whole plant or falling off of the entire crown.

Bunch rot is increasingly causing rotting of fruits before maturity among oil palm farmers in Uganda. The cause of the diseases has yet to be identified in Uganda but the major causes globally include *Marasmius palmivora* and "over bearing" in palms [12, 53]. Other diseases of oil palm identified in Uganda include; Leaf spot, Leaf rust, Anthracnose and Blast.

Oil palm weevil (*Rhyncophorus phoenicis*) is the most important pest of oil palm in Uganda responsible for fall of productive palms in all the oil palm producing blocks in Kalangala district [36]. Other pests of importance in Uganda include; Elephant beetle (*Augusoma centaurus*), and the Rhinoceros beetles (*Oryctes monoceros*). However, the larvae of the oil palm weevil are a delicacy in Kalangala and a significant source of accessible cash further complicating the management of the pest in the Island.

Research: Oil palm is a novel commercial crop in Uganda and as such, research is paramount in regard to identifying and addressing challenges associated with production of the crop in the country. Never the less, research in Uganda is tasked to develop local solutions to identified challenges given the dependency on foreign partners not only for seed but also locally untested best management practices. Research has thus considered the establishment of authorized nurseries in the country to ensure timely access to quality planting materials especially by resource limited farmers. This has ensured access to planting materials during the planting season and at the same time availability of locally tested and approved physiologically healthy genetically superior planting materials that will eventually boosting oil palm production. Without an active breeding program in the country, Uganda has imported a diversity of oil palm seedlings with varied genetic potential. Therefore, there is a need for an improved understanding by researchers on what type of oil palm varieties are essential for improvement. This can be done by first maintaining and conserving the genetic quality of existing yield generating varieties. Additional steps for controlling genetic quality might include the regulation and enforcement of standards, mass sensitization, and further research to establish characteristics which might allow early differentiation between hybrid and non-hybrid material as abasis for a breeding program in the country.

8. Future prospects for oil palm research in Uganda

The prospects for oil palm research are high in a similar way as the economic importance of the crop. The increasing demand for the oil palm products in the country, the information gap and the subsequent need to provide research solutions to sustain the oil palm industry in the country altogether will propel oil palm research in Uganda. Some of the areas that require attention which will provide useful information for increasing production and productivity in the oil palm sector include: Conducting fertilizer studies to establish the critical nutrient levels and fertilizer application rates for oil palm, determine the suitability of the different areas in the country for oil palm production, evaluate new materials for adaptation to potential areas identified for oil palm production, adopting locally customized research to establish some of the standards locally suitable in our environment such as planting distance, soil conservation and nutrient management under oil palm production, oil palm disease and pest identification and integrated management, regular farmer trainings to disseminate knowledge on better management and increased productivity, and locally applicable best management practices.

To the future, the oil palm research system should focus on production of hybrid varieties as they are more yielding and resistant to diseases. But because this requires technical steps including the selection of parents, inflorescence isolation, checking the inflorescence at maturity and controlled pollination, there is need for training of more oil palm researchers to work to contribute to the development of sustainable production of oil palm in the country.

Acknowledgements

Oil palm research in Uganda is spearheaded by the National Crop Resources Research Institute, NaCRRI, funded by the government of Uganda and International Fund for Agricultural Development, IFAD through the National Oil Palm Project, NOPP under the Ministry of Agriculture Animal Industry and Fisheries, MAAIF. Therefore, in a special way, we want to extend our sincere gratitude to the funders for the support offered in initiating oil palm research in Uganda, the administration of NaCRRI for their guidance in planning and management of project activities and finally to the Horticulture and oil palm research team for the energy and sacrifice they give in planning and implementing oil palm research activities.

Conflict of interest

We declare no conflict of interest.

Author details

Otuba Moses Amugoli*, Fred Bwayo Masika, Alex Asiimwe and Gabriel Ddamulira
National Crops Resources Research Institute (NaCRRI), National Agricultural Research Organization (NARO), Wakiso, Uganda

*Address all correspondence to: mozes.otuba@gmail.com

References

[1] Barcelos E, Rios S. d A, Cunha RNV, Lopes R, Motoike SY, et al. Oil palm natural diversity and the potential for yield improvement. Frontiers in Plant Science. 2015;**6**:190

[2] Jones LH, Hughes WA. Oil palm (Elaeis guineensis Jacq.). In Trees II. Berlin, Heidelberg: Springer; 1989. pp. 176-202

[3] Verheye W. Growth and Production of Oil Palm. In: Verheye W (ed.). Land Use, Land Cover and Soil Sciences. Encyclopedia of Life Support Systems (EOLSS). Oxford, UK: UNESCO-EOLSS Publishers; 2010. Available onlie: http://www.eolss.net

[4] Nambiappan B, Ismail A, Hashim N, Ismail N, Shahari DN, Idris NA, et al. Malaysia: 100 years of resilient palm oil economic performance. Journal of Oil Palm Research. Apr 2018;**30**(1):13-25

[5] Murphy DJ. The future of oil palm as a major global crop: Opportunities and challenges. Journal of Oil Palm Research. 1 Mar 2014;**26**(1):1-24

[6] Alam AF, Er AC, Begum H. Malaysian oil palm industry: Prospect and problem. Journal of Food, Agriculture and Environment. Apr 2015;**13**(2):143-148

[7] Hoyle D, Levang P. Oil Palm Development in Cameroon. An ad hoc working paper prepared by WWF, IRD and CIFOR; 2012

[8] Chew CL, Ng CY, Hong WO, Wu TY, Lee YY, Low LE, et al. Improving sustainability of palm oil production by increasing oil extraction rate: A review. Food and Bioprocess Technology. Apr 2021;**14**(4):573-586

[9] FAO. FAOSTAT. Food and Agriculture Organization of the United Nations, Rome, Italy; 2017. Available from: http://www.fao.org/faostat/en/#data

[10] Carrere R. Oil palm in Africa: Past, present and future scenarios. WRM series on tree plantations. Dec 2010;**15**(111):1-78

[11] Ddamulira G, Asiimwe A, Masika F, Amugoli M, Ddumba G, Nambuya A, Wetaala P, Maphosa M. Growth and Yield Parameters of Introduced Oil Palm Crop in Uganda. Journal of Agricultural Science. 2020;**12**(11)

[12] Masika FB, Danso I, Nangonzi R, Amugoli OM, Asiimwe A, Ddumba G, et al. Occurrence and severity of physiological disorders of oil palm (*Elaeis guineensis* Jacq. L.) in Uganda. Journal of Agricultural Science (Toronto). 2020;**12**(10):86-96

[13] NOPP (National Oil Palm Project). NOPP supervision report (Main report and annexes). National Oil Palm Project (NOPP), Project Number. 200000148, Republic of Uganda; 2020

[14] Corley RHV, Tinker PB. The Oil Palm. New York: John Wiley & Sons; 2016. http://dx.doi.org/10.1002/9781118953297

[15] Amugoli OM, Ddamulira G, Asiimwe A, Joseph K, Ddumba G, Mutyaba E, et al. Occurrence, distribution and farmers' knowledge on the management of fusarium wilt of oil palm among smallholders in Kalangala, Uganda. Journal of Oil Palm Research. 2020;**32**(3):488-496

[16] EPOA. The palm oil story. Zoetermeer, the Netherlands: European Palm Oil Alliance (EPOA). Retrieved 20 December 2018. Available from: https://www.palmoilandfood.eu/en

[17] Mielke T. Global Supply, Demand and Price Outlook of Oil & Fats in 2018/19. Global Market Research on Oilseeds, Oils and Meals. Hamburg, Germany: ISTA Mielke GmbH; 2018

[18] Ofosu-Budu K, Sarpong D. Oil palm industry growth in Africa: A value chain and smallholders' study for Ghana. In: Rebuilding West Africa's Food Potential, A. Elbehri (ed.), FAO/IFAD; 2013. pp. 349-389

[19] Jian Z, Wang C, Dai J, Chen X, Ge K. Palm oil diet may benefit mildly hypercholesterolaemic Chinese adults. Asia Pacific Journal of Clinical Nutrition. 1997;**6**:22-25

[20] Zhang J, Ping W, Chunrong W, Shou CX, Keyou G. Nonhyper-cholesterolemic effects of a palm oil diet in Chinese adults. The Journal of Nutrition. 1 Mar 1997;**127**(3): 509S-513S

[21] Truswell AS, Choudhury N, Roberts CK. Double blind comparison of plasma lipids in Healthy subjects eating potato crisps fried in palm olein of canola oil. Journal of Food Technology in Africa. 1999;**4**(2)

[22] Sundram K, Hornstra G, Houwelingen AC, Kester AD. Replacement of dietary fat with palm oil: Effect on human serum lipids, lipoproteins and apolipoproteins. The British Journal of Nutrition. Nov 1992;**68**(3):677-692

[23] Corley RH. How much palm oil do we need? Environmental Science & Policy. 1 Apr 2009;**12**(2):134-139

[24] Rosillo-Calle F, Pelkmans L, Walter A. A global overview of vegetable oils, with reference to biodiesel. A report for the IEA Bioenergy Task. 2009. pp. 40

[25] Sulaiman O, Salim N, Nordin NA, Hashim R, Ibrahim M, Sato M. The potential of oil palm trunk biomass as an alternative source for compressed wood. BioResources. 2 May 2012;7(2):2688-2706

[26] Sumathi S, Chai SP, Mohamed AR. Utilization of oil palm as a source of renewable energy in Malaysia. Renewable and Sustainable Energy Reviews. 2008 Dec 1;**12**(9):2404-2421

[27] Kelly-Yong TL, Lee KT, Mohamed AR, Bhatia S. Potential of hydrogen from oil palm biomass as a source of renewable energy worldwide. Energy Policy. 1 Nov 2007;**35**(11):5692-5701

[28] Sayer J, Ghazoul J, Nelson P, Boedhihartono AK. Oil palm expansion transforms tropical landscapes and livelihoods. Global Food Security. 1 Dec 2012;**1**(2):114-119

[29] Rival A, Levang P. Palms of Controversies: Oil Palm and Development Challenges. Bogor, Indonesia: CIFOR; 1 Jul 2014

[30] Nkongho RN, Feintrenie L, Levang P. The Non-Industrial Palm Oil Sector in Cameroon. Working Paper 139. Bogor, Indonesia: CIFOR; 15 Jul 2014

[31] NOPP (National Oil Palm Project). Final project design report (Main report and annexes). National Oil Palm Project (NOPP), Project No. 2000001484, Republic of Uganda; 2017

[32] Oh E. "Getting the genome to work". The Star. 16 May 2009. p. SBW24

[33] Woittiez LS, Van Wijk MT, Slingerland M, Van Noordwijk M, Giller KE. Yield gaps in oil palm: A quantitative review of contributing factors. European Journal of Agronomy. Feb 2017;**1**(83):57-77

[34] Sparnaaij LD. The analysis of bunch production in the oil palm [thesis]. Promotor(en): C. Coolhaas. Wageningen University

[35] Combres JC, Pallas B, Rouan L, Mialet-Serra I, Caliman JP, Braconnier S, et al. Simulation of inflorescence dynamics in oil palm and estimation of environment-sensitive phenological phases: A model based analysis. Functional Plant Biology. 12 Nov 2012;**40**(3):263-279

[36] Baguma J, Otema M, Ddamulira G, Naluyimba R, Egonyu JP. Distribution and incidence of the oil palm weevil *Rhynchophorus phoenicis* (Fabricius, 1801) (Coleoptera: Curculionidae) in selected agro-ecological zones of Uganda. African Entomology: Journal of the Entomological Society of Southern Africa. 1 Sep 2019;**27**(2):477-487

[37] Faleiro JR, Al-Shuaibi MA, Abraham VA, Kumar TP. A technique to assess the longevity of the pheromone (Ferrolure) used in trapping the date red palm weevil *Rhynchophorous ferrugineus* Oliv. Journal of Agricultural and Marine Sciences [JAMS]. 1 Jan 1999;**4**(1):5-9

[38] Carr MK. The water relations and irrigation requirements of oil palm (Elaeis guineensis): A review. Experimental Agriculture. Oct 2011;**47**(4):629-652

[39] Smith BG. The effects of soil water and atmospheric vapour pressure deficit on stomatal behaviour and photosynthesis in the oil palm. Journal of Experimental Botany. 1 Jun 1989;**40**(6):647-651

[40] Caliman JP. Oil palm and water deficit: Production, adapted cultural techniques. Oléagineux (Paris). 1992;**47**(5):205-216

[41] Henson IE, Chang KC. Evidence for water as a factor limiting performance of field palms in West Malaysia. In Proceedings of 1989 PORIM International Palm Oil Development Conference–Agriculture; Palm Oil Research Institute of Malaysia, Kuala Lumpur; 1990. pp. 487-498

[42] FAOSTAT. 2015. [Internet] Available from: http://www.fao.org/nr/water/aquastat/countries_regions/UGA/

[43] Jacquemard JC. Le palmier à huile. Torrossa, ID: 5063401. Le palmier à huile. 2011. pp. 1-240

[44] Funk C, Rowland J, Eilerts G, White L, Martin TE, Maron JL. A climate trend analysis of Uganda. US Geological Survey Fact Sheet 2012-3062. 2012(4)

[45] Samedani B, Juraimi AS, Rafii MY, Sheikh Awadz SA, Anwar MP, Anuar AR. Effect of cover crops on weed suppression in oil palm plantation. International Journal of Agriculture and Biology. 30 Apr 2015;**17**(2):251-260

[46] Adaigbe VC, Imogie AE, Edokpayi AA. Effect of weed on oil palm inflorescence production: Implication on *Elaeidobius kamerunicus* population. Journal of Agriculture, Forestry and the Social Sciences. 2006;**4**(2):89-91

[47] Marcelino JP, Diaz EV. Effect of frond pruning on the growth and yield of oil palm. Philippine Journal of Crop Science (Philippines). 2010;**35**:33

[48] Corley RH, Tinker PB. The Oil Palm. UK: John Willey and Sons. Blackwell Science; 18 Apr 2008

[49] Paul TC. Fusarium wilt of oil palm: Studies on resistance and pathogenicity [thesis]. United Kingdom: University of Bath; 1995

[50] Prendergast AG. Observations on the epidemiology of vascular wilt disease of the Oil Palm (*Elaeis guineensis*, Jacq.). Journal of the West African Institute for Oil Palm Research. 1957;**2**(6)

[51] Turner PD. The incidence of Ganoderma disease of oil palms in Malaya and its relation to previous crop. Annals of Applied Biology. Jun 1965;**55**(3):417-423

[52] Bull RA. Studies on the deficiency diseases of the oil palm: I. Orange Frond Disease caused by magnesium deficiency. Journal of the West African Institute for Oil Palm Research. 1954;**2**:94-129

[53] Turner PD, Bull RA. Diseases and disorders of the oil palm in Malaysia. In: Diseases and Disorders of the Oil Palm in Malaysia. Incorporated Society of Planters, Kuala Lumpur, Malaysia. 1967. pp. 247

Chapter 5

Small-Scale Palm Oil Production in Ghana: Practices, Environmental Problems and Potential Mitigating Measures

Eric Awere, Alessandra Bonoli, Peter Appiah Obeng, Sara Pennellini, Sara Bottausci, William Kwaasi Amanor and Emmanuel Kekeli Akuaku

Abstract

The environmental impact of small-scale palm oil processing mills in Ghana has come under serious questioning, especially the disposal of wastewater generated from their operations. This chapter describes the small-scale palm oil production operations in Ghana to highlight the associated environmental problems arising from the disposal of wastewater and other waste by-products. The chapter further discusses the effluent discharge permitting arrangements and possible modifications to the production practices and policy interventions that could improve their environmental compliance and encourage resource recovery. The data in this chapter was obtained from a survey of selected small-scale palm oil processing mills in Ghana, laboratory analysis of wastewater samples from processing mills and review of related literature. Wastewater generated from the processing activities is currently disposed of without any form of treatment. The characteristics of wastewater indicate the need for treatment before disposal. Treatment technologies that could achieve resource recovery (such as biogas, compost, earthworm biomass) and fit into the framework of circular economy should be explored.

Keywords: Ghana, environmental impacts, palm oil production, palm oil mill wastewater, small-scale processing mills

1. Introduction

1.1 Background information

Palm oil is largely produced in Asia, Africa, and Latin America. However, the origin is traced to the tropical rain forest and equatorial region of Africa. Whereas oil palm is traced to Africa, 2019 data suggests that palm oil production as a

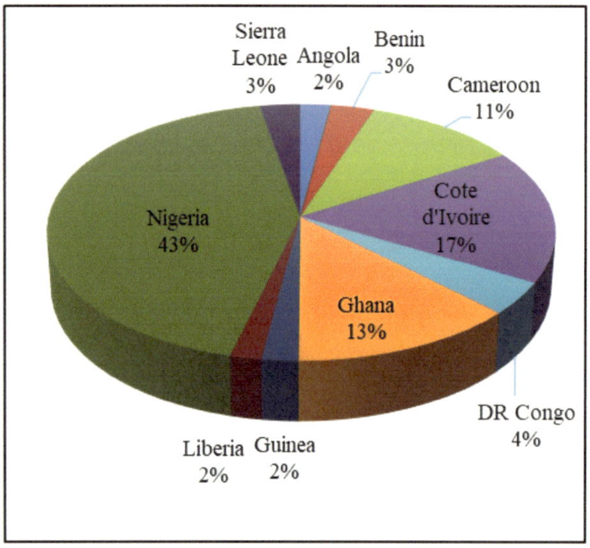

Figure 1.
Proportion of palm oil production in Africa, 2019. Data from FAOSTAT [1].

percentage of the global output was only about 3% for West Africa and 4% for Africa [1]. The major palm oil production countries in Africa are Nigeria (43%), Cote d'lvoire (17%), Ghana (13%) and Cameroon (11%). **Figure 1** shows the proportion of Africa's 2019 palm oil production by country. This does not include countries with less than 2% output.

Palm oil is the most important edible oil in Ghana and in the West Africa region. Palm oil and palm kernel represented 2% of total agricultural production value of Ghana in 2010 [2]. The processing of oil palm is a major source of income and employment to many women in the rural areas of the forest agroecological zone [3]. By 2015, the palm oil production sector was employing over 2 million people mostly in rural areas [4]. Crude palm oil, particularly those produced by the small-scale industry of Ghana, is used as vegetable oil in many local cuisines. Data from the 2008 Ghana Demographic and Health Survey shows that one out of every two households (54%) in the country and four out of five (80%) households in the Central Region used palm oil in food preparation [5]. From analysis of palm oil production and consumption in Ghana between the year 2005 and 2010, Angelucci [2] reported that the country produced a total of 120,000 tonnes of palm oil. As at 2021, the country's crude palm oil production had increased to 375,000 tonnes [6], doubling the production in a decade. The trend of palm oil production in Ghana from 2000 to 2021 is presented in **Figure 2**. However, Ghana has an annual production deficit of about 30,000 tonnes which is estimated to reach 127,000 tonnes by 2024 [7].

Suitable conditions for oil palm cultivation exist in the wetter southern part [8] in the rainforest and semi-deciduous forest zones. Based on the agro-ecological zones, palm oil has a wide national geographical coverage as it is cultivated in nine (9) out of the sixteen (16) first level administrative regions of Ghana. The most suitable areas for oil palm cultivation are said to be the Ahafo, Ashanti, Bono, Bono East, Central, Eastern, Oti, Western, and Western North Regions [8].

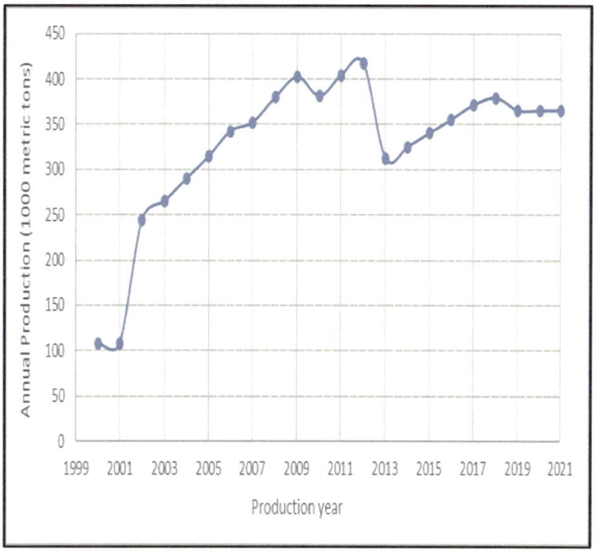

Figure 2.
Annual crude palm oil production of Ghana, 2000-2021. Data from IndexMundi [6]

1.2 Overview of imports and exports of palm oil in Ghana

Ghana is a net importer of crude palm oil even though the country exports crude palm oil to other neighboring West African countries such as Senegal, Benin, Burkina Faso, Nigeria, and Niger [9]. There has been a steady increase in exports and imports of crude palm oil, but the trend is not consistent. **Figure 3** shows the trend of trade value of palm oil imports and exports for Ghana from 2005 to 2019.

Imports of crude palm oil reached 119,821 MT with a trade value of US$ 57.2million (**Figure 3**) in 2019. Countries from where Ghana imports palm oil are mainly Malaysia, Indonesia, Cote d'lvoire, Liberia, Singapore and Togo [9]. On the other hand, exports for 2019 was significantly lower with only 15,392 MT with a trade value of US$ 11.1million, about one-fifth of the import value. For most of the years, imports were higher than exports except for 2012 and 2013 when crude palm oil exports far exceeded (31–69 times) the imports. Within the past one-half decades (i.e., 2005–2019), there has been substantial imports of crude palm oil to meet domestic and industrial needs. From 2005 to 2019, Ghana imported about 1.1 million metric tonnes of crude palm oil with a trade value of about US$ 1.2billion. However, export quantity (in MT) within the same period was only about 18% of the total imports.

1.3 Palm oil processing characteristics

Palm oil is processed from fresh fruits using various techniques that differ in the level of mechanization and interconnecting material transfer mechanisms. The scale of operations also differs at the level of processing. Palm oil processing in Ghana (like other West African countries) is undertaken by four (4) distinct groups of actors [10]. These actors, according to their throughput and degree of complexity, are traditional, small-scale,

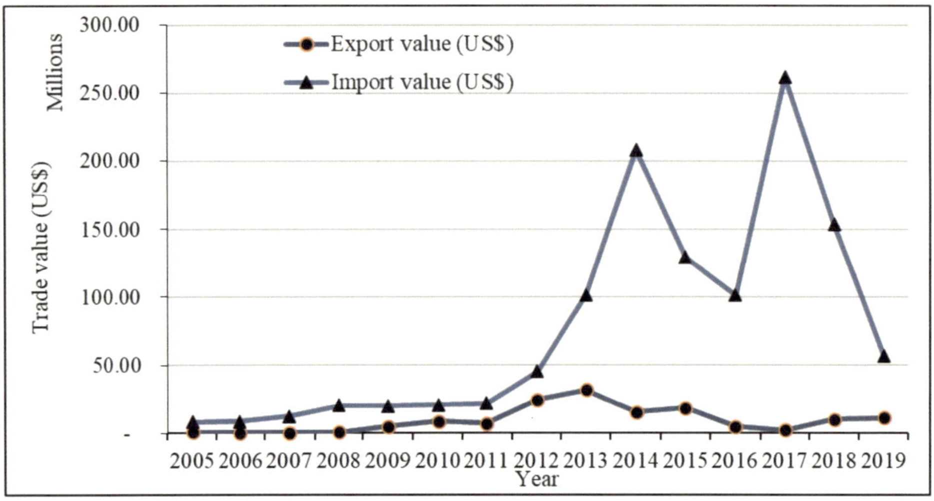

Figure 3.
Trade value of export and import of crude palm oils, Ghana (2005–2019).

medium-scale and large-scale mills. In terms of the level of complexity, the traditional producers use methods which are basically manual with the use of rudimentary tools. The small-scale producers use a variety of low-efficiency machinery ranging from simple hand presses and other stand-alone machines to a very varied combination of machines which cater for the various unit processes in the production cycle. In terms of throughput, small-scale processing units handle up to 2 tonnes per hour

Characteristic	Large-scale Mills	Medium-scale Mills	Small-scale Mills	Artisanal Mills
Annual Production (FFB in tonnes)	70,000 – 140,000	15,000 – 30,000	2000–5000	2–70
Oil Extraction Rates (%)	16–23	12–15	12–13	8–10
Material Handling	Fully mechanized system in sequential processing steps	Semi mechanized system with few manual interventions	Semi mechanized system with more manual interventions	Manual process
Technology	Intermediate	Intermediate	Low	Very low
Labour	High skilled artisans and labour	Mix of skilled and unskilled labour	Mainly unskilled labour	Laborious and unskilled.
Environment	Compliant with EPA regulations and members of RSPO	Non-compliant with EPA	Non-compliant with EPA	Non-compliant with EPA

Source: MASDAR [11].

Table 1.
Scale of palm oil processing mills in Ghana and their characteristics.

of fresh fruit bunches (FFB) [10, 11]. The medium-scale and large-scale mills have technologically up-to-date machinery, established by agro-industrial complexes for the production of palm oil [12] with production throughput of up to 60 tonnes of FFB per hour. Characteristics of the different palm oil mills in Ghana is summarized in **Table 1**.

Though small-scale producers are characterized by weak milling capacity and low quality crude palm oil produced [13, 14] they occupy a greater share of the palm oil processing industry. Available data shows that there were more than 1200 small-scale mills in Ghana [11] producing 60–80% of the national palm oil production [2, 15]. By 2015, the small-scale industry was employing over 2 million people [4] mostly in rural areas.

2. The problem and contribution of the chapter

There are reports of the discharge of raw palm oil mill wastewater into the environment [15, 16]. The Master Plan study on the Palm Oil Industry in Ghana revealed that the activities of small-scale palm oil processers do not comply with environmental regulations [11]. The limited data on the characteristics of wastewater produced by small-scale mills in Ghana casts shadow on the level of environmental damage caused by this important subsector of the economy. This, in turn, obscures the possible technical and policy interventions that may be proffered to mitigate the environmental impacts of the industry. The informal and wide-spread nature and high contribution of small-scale mills to Ghana's palm oil production warrant attention and research.

This chapter describes the small-scale palm oil production operations in Ghana to highlight the associated environmental problems arising from the disposal of wastewater and other waste by-products. The chapter further discusses the effluent discharge permitting arrangements and possible modifications to the production practices and policy interventions that could improve their environmental compliance and encourage resource recovery.

3. Chapter methods

3.1 The study area and selection of production mills

The study was conducted in the Central Region of Ghana, which is one of the sixteen (16) first-level government administrative units of Ghana. There is only one functional large-scale palm oil processing plant in the Central Region. This affords small-scale mills the opportunity for greater access to oil palm for processing. Twenty-five (25) small-scale processing mills were selected from four (4) palm oil processing Metropolitan, Municipal and District Assemblies (MMDA) namely Cape Coast Metropolitan Area (CCMA), Abura Aseibu Kwamankese District (AAKD), Twifo Hemang Lower Denkyira District (THLDD) and Mfantseman Municipality (MfM) all in the Central region of Ghana. The MMDAs were strategically selected to ensure agro-ecological balance (forest zone, transition zone, and coastal savanna zone). A map showing the study area and location of the selected small-scale processing mills is presented in **Figure 4**.

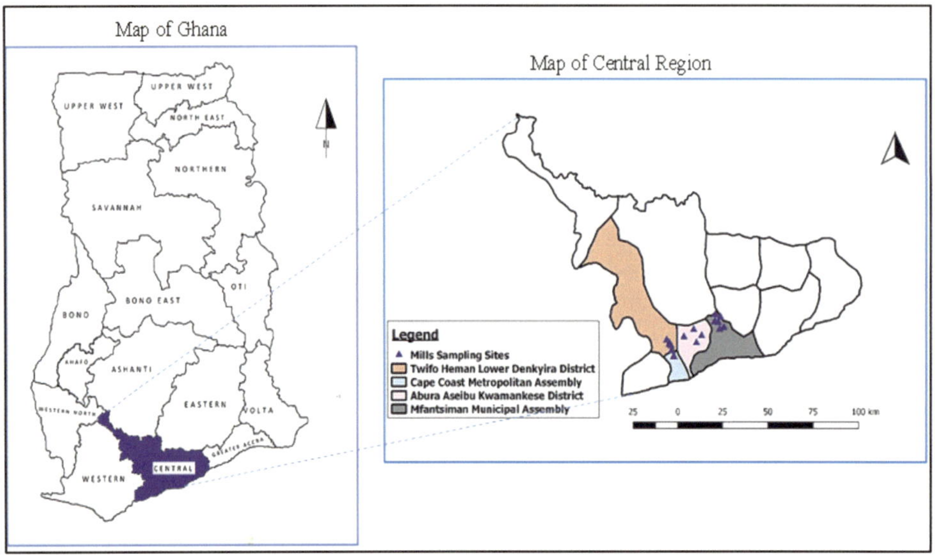

Figure 4.
Map of the study area and sampling location.

3.2 Data collection methods

Data for this chapter was collected through interviews, structured observations, and review of relevant literature. An interview guide was designed and pre-tested (using eight small-scale palm oil processers in the Twifo Atti Morkwa District, Central Region of Ghana) for use in the study. For each of the processing mills, the manager/mill operator and a worker/processer were interviewed using the interview guide. The structured observation technique was employed to corroborate the information obtained from the mill operators through the interviews.

3.3 Wastewater characterization

Wastewater samples were collected from four (4) small-scale palm oil processing mills from Abura Aseibu Kwamankese District in the Central Region of Ghana. Samples were taken from each of the processing mills during the lean palm oil production season (August 2019) and peak production season (March 2020). For each of the processing mills and in each season, samples of wastewater were collected separately from boiling and clarification tanks. Samples were collected in opaque plastic containers and labeled appropriately before transport to the Environmental Quality Engineering laboratory of the Cape Coast Technical University, Ghana for analysis.

The following parameters were measured: pH, total solids (TS), total suspended solids (TSS), total dissolved solids (TDS), chemical oxygen demand (COD), biochemical oxygen demand (BOD_5), total nitrogen, phosphorus, potassium and oil and grease. The pH measurements were performed using Portable pH-meters XS Series. The solids content was determined using the gravimetric method. Fats and oils were determined using the Soxhlet extraction method. All the remaining parameters were analyzed using Hanna multiparameter photometer (HI83399) and associated reagents. Analysis was carried out according to Standard analytical methods prescribed by Standard Methods for Examination of Water and Wastewater [17]. All analysis was performed in triplicates and the mean value taken.

3.4 Assessment of processing practices and wastewater management

The processing practices for palm oil production and wastewater management practices employed by the processing mills were obtained through the interviews and structured observation. Moreover, reasons for the wastewater management practices at the processing mills were ascertained through the interviews.

4. Results and discussion

4.1 Palm oil production processes in Ghana

The production processes used in the study area generally reflect what is employed in other parts of Ghana. The processing of fresh palm fruits into crude palm oil involves receipt of fresh fruit bunches, splitting, storage, stripping, fermentation, boiling, digestion/pressing and clarification. The only mechanized operations are digestion and/or pressing of boiled fruits as noted by other authors [15, 18]. However, fermentation of fresh or boiled fruits is an optional activity which is used depending on the expected grade (food or soap) of the crude palm oil produced. **Table 2** describes the production processes employed by the small-scale processing mills in the Central Region of Ghana. The corresponding process flow diagram is shown in **Figure 5**.

4.2 Environmental regulations for palm oil processing mills in Ghana

4.2.1 Environmental permitting

Palm oil processing mills (small-, medium- and large-scale) are required under Regulation 1 of the Ghana Environmental Assessment Regulations, 1999 (LI 1652) to register with and obtain environmental permit from the Ghana Environmental Protection Agency (EPA) prior to the commencement of the undertaking. In addition, existing undertakings, where EPA considers to have or is likely to have adverse effect on the environment or public health, are required to register with and obtain environmental permit in respect of the undertaking. Similarly, the Environmental Protection Agency Act, 1994 (Act 490) authorizes the EPA "to issue environmental permits and pollution abatement notices for controlling the volume, types, constituents and effects of waste discharges, emissions, deposits or any other source of pollutants and of substances which are hazardous or potentially dangerous to the quality of the environment or a segment of the environment."

The Ghana EPA is therefore legally mandated to regulate and enforce all environmental laws and regulations. But, the small-scale processing mills belong to the informal sector where compliance to legal requirements has been noted to be relatively weak [22, 23]. The economic activities (in law and practice) of small-scale mills are not or insufficiently covered by formal arrangements including registration and regulation [23]. This is confirmed by Gyamfi [24] that 70% of respondents from small-scale mills in Ashanti, Eastern, Central and Western regions of Ghana were

Unit operation	Processing practices
Receipt of fresh fruit bunches	The fresh fruit bunches are brought to the mills in baskets or in small trucks. Harvesting, postharvest transportation and handling of fresh fruit bunches at the small-scale mills lead to much of the fruits been bruised [10].
Splitting of bunches	The FFBs are divided into small parts (splitting /quartering) using cutlass or ax. The aim is to obtain smaller sizes for easy handling during stripping. This activity is mostly performed by men. Splitting or quartering is done on the bare ground which leads to fruit bruises.
Storage	The quartered/split bunches are stored on the bare floor with or without covering for up to 6 days. A storage duration of 3-7 days have been reported in other areas [15, 18, 19, 20]. Materials mostly used for covering are palm fronds, jute bags or plastic sheets. The aim of this activity is to allow enough time for the tissue holding the fruit and bunches together to wilt and facilitate loosening of the fruits from the bunches. However, storage allows the formation of free fatty acids (FFA) which affects the quality of the crude palm oil produced. To some extent, storage also reduces the moisture content of the fruits [18].
Stripping/ loosening	The fruits are manually separated from the bunches using sticks, blunt side of cutlasses or handpicking. The stripping equipment used further leads to fruit bruising. The waste product from this operation is fresh empty fruit bunches (FFB).
Fermentation (optional)	The loosened fresh fruits are heaped in baskets for 3–10 days (used in the study area) or 1–4 weeks as reported by others [15, 18] to allow fermentation to take place. The duration of storage depends on the end-use of the crude palm oil (food-grade or soap-grade). For food-grade oils, fermentation period does not exceed 1 week [22]. On the other hand, for soap-grade oil, the boiled fruits are fermented for 2–5 days to reduce the moisture content before pressing [21].
Boiling	The fermented or unfermented fruits are submerged in water in metal drums or cooking pots and boiled over open fires. The fires are set and maintained by using firewood, dried coconut branches, dried empty palm fruit bunches and palm pressed fiber. The use of waste car tires to set the fire has been reported in other areas [15]. During boiling, the fruits are covered with jute bags or palm fronds to minimize heat loss. Boiling takes 1–2 hours. The objectives of fruit boiling, according to Poku [10] are to: • Deactivate the enzymes responsible for free fatty acid (FFA) build-up • Soften and prepare the fruit mesocarp for digestion • Detach kernels from the shells and to prevent the kernels from breaking during pressing The fire produces smoke which could affect the health of processers. In addition, processers are exposed to heat during manual scooping and transfer of fruits to the digester. The waste product from boiling is boiler wastewater, smoke and ash.
Digestion	This is one of the mechanized operations. The boiled fruits are manually scooped and conveyed into a mechanical digester. The digestion process breaks the exocarp and oil-bearing mesocarp to enhance oil extraction. This operation is undertaken while the boiled fruits are still hot in order to reduce the viscosity of the oil [10]. The most common mechanical digesters in use are horizontal and vertical digesters [20].
Oil extraction and clarification	Extraction of oil is accomplished using mechanical presses. The process separates the oil from the mash. Depending on the required quality of the oil, two methods of oil extraction exist, i.e., 'dry' and 'wet'. The dry method uses mechanical presses to squeeze out the oil. The oil produced from the dry method is mostly soap-grade. In the wet method, the boiled fruits are squeezed to produce a mixture of oil, cell debris, fibrous materials, and water. Hot water is added, and the mixture is then kept on fire under low heat for 1–2 hours for the oil to flow to the surface. The clear oil is skimmed manually from the surface into a storage tank. Food-grade oil is produced from the wet method. The waste products are pressed cake which comprises of palm pressed fiber, palm kernels and clarification wastewater.

Table 2.
Description of small-scale palm oil production processes in Ghana.

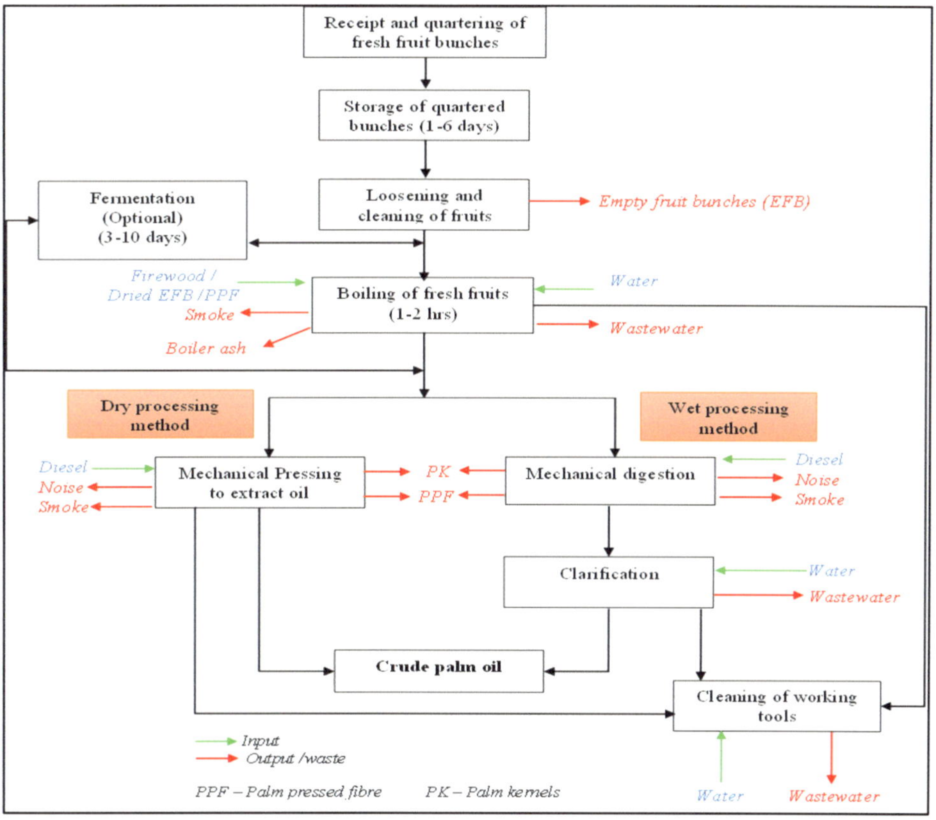

Figure 5.
Process flow diagram for palm oil processing at small-scale level. Source: Authors.

either not aware of or did not know how to comply with national environmental laws and regulations.

4.2.2 Effluent standards for palm oil mill industry in Ghana

Wastewater produced by the palm oil processing mills are required to be treated to meet the Ghana Environmental Protection – Requirements for Effluent Discharge (GS 1212:2019) Standard [25] promulgated by the Ghana Standards Authority. The Standard specifies the requirements for sector specific effluent quality and gives guidelines for discharge of effluents into the environment. **Table 3** shows the effluent discharge standard for oil and fat processing which includes the palm oil industry.

4.3 Characteristics of wastewater from Central Region of Ghana

4.3.1 Composite characteristics of palm oil mill wastewater

The composite characteristics of wastewater from the small-scale palm oil processing in Central Region of Ghana are summarized in **Table 4** compared with the Ghana effluent discharge standard, characteristics of palm oil mill wastewater from

Parameter	Unit	Standard
Color	TCU	300
Temperature	°C	≤3 above Ambient
pH	—	6–9
TDS	mg/L	1000
TSS	mg/L	50
BOD_5	mg/L	50
COD	mg/L	250
Oil and grease	mg/L	10
Pesticides, Total	mg/L	0.5
Phosphorus, Total	mg/L	2
Coliforms, Total	MPN/100 ml	400

Oil and fat processing industry includes oil and palm, shear butter, peanuts, coconut oil, palm kernel, etc. Source: GSA [25].

Table 3.
Effluent standard for oil and fat processing industry in Ghana.

Parameter	Central Region, Ghana	Iwuagwu and Ugwuanyi [26]	Wood, Pillai [27]	Ghana effluent discharge standard
pH	4.61–4.74	3.9	—	6–9
TS	2569-5327	76,000	29,600-55,400	
TDS	211–551	32,000	15,500-59,000	1000
TSS	2070-5106	44,000	14,100-26,400	50
BOD_5	16,172-27,888	—	17,000-26,700	50
COD	50,391-60,544	114,800	42,900-88,250	250
Total Nitrogen	160–373	420	500–800	—
Phosphorus	43–90	—	94–131	—
Potassium	126–191	—	1281-1928	2
Oil and grease	321–792	—	4400-8000	10

All values are in mg/l except pH.
TS-total solids; TDS-total dissolved solids; TSS-total suspended solids.
Figures in bold are outside the Ghana effluent discharge limits.

Table 4.
Characteristics of palm oil mill wastewater from small-scale mills in the Central Region of Ghana and literature.

small-scale processing mill in Nigeria and a large-scale mill in Malaysia. The wastewater contained solids, oxygen-consuming compounds, nutrients (nitrogen, phosphorus and potassium) and oil and grease. Around 13–22% of the total solids and 20–23% of suspended solids were in the form of oil and grease.

The COD:BOD_5 was 2.1–3.1 (mean = 2.5) indicating the presence of slowly biodegradable organic matter as noted by Henze, van Loosdrecht [28]. This may be attributed largely to the unrecovered fats and oils in the wastewater as noted by Cisterna-Osorio and Arancibia-Avila [29]. It has been reported that, slowly biodegradable COD constitutes 45% of the total COD of raw palm oil mill wastewater with only about 20% being readily biodegradable due to the free fatty acids [30]. Low pH of wastewater from palm oil processing is also due to the organic acids formed during fermentation of the palm fruits [31]. The acidity of palm oil and, by extension, the palm oil mill wastewater have been reported to be affected by the extraction procedure, presence of microorganisms and the genotype of the palm tree [32]. Suspended solids in the wastewater consists of carbohydrates with oil and other organic and inorganic solids [27]. Most of these solid constituents could serve as nutrient sources for microorganisms.

4.3.2 Seasonal characteristics of palm oil mill wastewater

The wastewater characteristics varied with production season (see **Table 5**). The characteristics of wastewater produced during the peak season were generally higher than the lean season except for pH and solids (total and suspended). Irrespective of the production season, the wastewater was characterized by slowly biodegradable organic matter ($COD:BOD_5$ = 2.5–2.6).

Boiling and clarification time during the lean season are mostly greater than the peak season due to lower processing cycles. A longer clarification time corresponds to greater oil extraction rate, higher evaporation, lower moisture content and higher solids in the wastewater. This reflects the higher concentration of solids in wastewater produced during the lean season as compared to the peak season. The differences in the mean pH, TDS and total nitrogen were significant at 1% level. Potassium concentration in the peak season was significantly higher than the lean season at 3% level. The seasonal variation for TS, TSS, BOD_5, COD, Phosphorus and oil & grease were statistically insignificant. It could be deduced from the results that similar organic and solid loading rates may be used for designing treatment system to handle wastewater for both the peak and lean seasons.

Parameter	**Mean (SD)**		**Seasonal differences** [a] **(*p*-value)**
	Peak season	**Lean season**	
pH	4.17 (0.23)	4.65 (0.05)	−0.48 (*0.000*)**
TS	3419 (1381)	3976 (1397)	−557 (*0.436*)
TDS	1107 (431)	358 (158)	749 (*0.001*)**
TSS	2313 (962)	3618 (1551)	−1305 (*0.066*)
BOD_5	23,803 (3766)	21,877 (4728)	1926 (*0.384*)
COD	58,948 (5370)	56,357 (3441)	2591 (*0.273*)
Total nitrogen	377 (40)	246 (86)	131 (*0.003*)**
Phosphorus	60 (16)	49 (24)	11 (*0.325*)
Potassium	188 (28)	156 (24)	32 (*0.026*)*
Oil and grease	628 (389)	527 (198)	101 (*0.527*)

All values are in mg/l except pH. [a]*Peak season minus lean season.*
**Significant at 3% level.*
***Significant at 1% level.*
Source: Authors.

Table 5.
Seasonal characteristics of palm oil mill wastewater.

4.3.3 Characteristics of different wastewater streams

The characteristics of the wastewater from boiling and clarification sampled during the peak and lean production seasons are presented in **Table 6**. For both production seasons, the pH, TDS, BOD_5 and COD of the wastewater from boiling were higher than for clarification. For the remaining parameters (TS, TSS, oil & grease, total nitrogen, phosphorus and potassium) the clarification wastewater was higher than the wastewater from boiling. Apart from BOD_5 and COD, the trend of the results was consistent with the characteristics of individual wastewater streams reported in Malaysia.

The COD:BOD_5 was 2.3–2.4 for wastewater from boiling and 2.6–3.1 for wastewater from clarification. The biodegradability of the wastewater from boiling would be better than the wastewater from clarification. The higher COD:BOD_5 for wastewater from clarification compared to boiling may be attributed to the higher fat and oil content of the wastewater from clarification. The differences in the mean concentration of parameters between boiling and clarification were statistically significant at 1–2% level.

Parameter	Peak season			Lean season		
	Mean (SD)		p-value	Mean (SD)		p-value
	Boiling	Clarification		Boiling	Clarification	
pH	4.36 (0.08)	3.98 (0.13)	*0.054*	4.67 (0.05)	4.62 (0.01)	*0.125*
TS	2130 (82)	4708 (81)	*0.000***	2670 (68)	5282 (40)	*0.000***
TDS	1420 (55)	503 (113)	*0.001***	2168 (84)	214 (4.8)	*0.002***
TSS	710 (27)	4205 (179)	*0.000***	502 (54)	5068 (36)	*0.000***
BOD_5	26,672 (3050)	20,935 (1358)	*0.026**	26,196 (1211)	17,559 (971)	*0.000***
COD	63,503 (2867)	54,392 (1932)	*0.003***	59,141 (1297)	53,572 (2295)	*0.008***
Total nitrogen	362 (3.1)	393 (55)	*0.339*	170 (7.1)	321 (44)	*0.006***
Phosphorus	29 (8.1)	69 (12)	*0.003***	46 (2.2)	73 (11)	*0.018**
Potassium	163 (5.4)	214 (7.1)	*0.000***	136 (12)	175 (13)	*0.005***
Oil and grease	276 (19)	980 (147)	*0.003***	358 (35)	695 (119)	*0.006***

*All values are in mg/l except pH. *Significant at 5% level.*
***Significant at 1% level.*
Source: Authors.

Table 6.
Characteristics of wastewater from boiling and clarification for peak and lean production seasons.

4.4 Wastewater management practices and potential environmental impacts

4.4.1 Wastewater management practices in the Central Region of Ghana

Assessment of the twenty-five (25) small-scale processing mills revealed that none of the mills had a wastewater treatment facility. Consequently, untreated wastewater generated from the extraction processes were discharged on the land or through drains to nearby bushes (**Figure 6**).

Similar environmentally unfriendly wastewater disposal practices by small scale mills have been reported in Nigeria [16]. Contrary to other observations [15], none of the mills assessed in this study disposed their wastewater directly into streams or rivers. Nevertheless, in all the mills assessed, the areas where wastewater was disposed had lost their vegetation. This confirms observations in Africa by Poku [10] that the bushes near the small-scale mills where wastewater is disposed die slowly. Moreover, a very strong stench characterizes the processing mills possibly due to the decomposing wastewater.

4.4.2 Reasons for current wastewater management practices in Central Region, Ghana

The reasons ascribed by the processing mills for disposal of untreated wastewater in the natural environment are presented in **Figure 7**.

All the operators of the processing mills are aware of the legal requirement to treat the wastewater generated by their activities. However, majority (48%) of the operators blamed the absence of treatment system on their limited technical capacity on wastewater management. Others (36%) do not have the financial resources to construct and manage a treatment facility. Finally, few processing mills took advantage of limited enforcement of environmental regulations by the relevant Government Agency (Ghana Environmental Protection Agency) to dispose of their wastewater without treatment. Comparatively, a study conducted by Gyamfi [24] revealed that 70% of respondents from small-scale mills in Ashanti, Eastern, Central and Western

Figure 6.
Wastewater disposal practices at small-scale palm oil processing mills in the Central Region of Ghana (source: Authors).

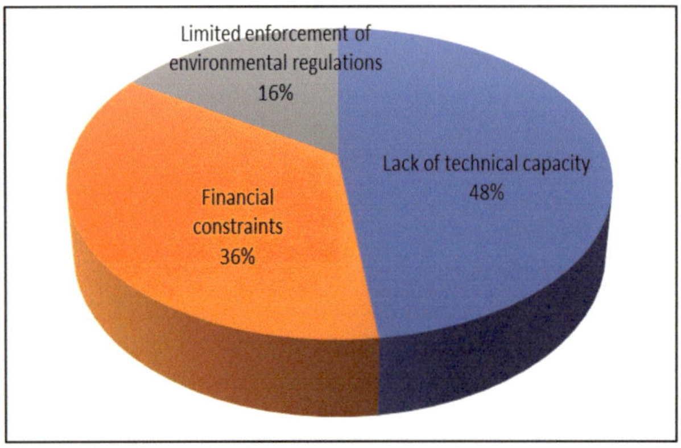

Figure 7.
Reasons for absence of wastewater treatment facilities at small-scale processing mills in the Central Region of Ghana. (source: Authors).

regions of Ghana were either not aware or did not know how to comply with national environmental laws and regulations. The economic activities (in law or practice) of small-scale mills are not or insufficiently covered by formal arrangements including registration and regulation [23].

4.4.3 Potential environmental impacts of current wastewater management practices

The concentrations of most of the parameters were over 2-order of magnitude higher than the limits set by Ghana Standards Authority (see **Table 4**). Palm-oil extraction wastewater disposed on land could be washed into surface water bodies by runoff. When washed into water bodies, the high organic content of the wastewater could deplete the oxygen content of the receiving water bodies [33, 34] and affect the life of their aquatic organisms [35]. Using a per capita BOD loading of 54 gBOD/day [36], the population equivalent (PE) of the small-scale industry is about 200 inhabitants. Excessive fats and oils may form scum [37] on the surface of waterbodies further depriving the water body of dissolved oxygen.

Moreover, the untreated wastewater pollutes the air through odor production as reported by Ahmad and Ghufran [38] and Loh, Lai [39]. Aside the odor, the degradation of the wastewater could generate biogas with over 60% methane content [39, 40]. Methane gas is considered one of the potent greenhouse gases and contributes 25 times to global warming compared to CO_2 [41]. The current practice of disposing raw wastewater into the natural environment by small-scale processing mills is negatively affecting the environment.

4.5 Other palm-oil extraction waste products and their management in Ghana

4.5.1 Solid waste

The categories of solid waste generated at the processing mills are empty fruit bunches (EFB), palm pressed fiber, palm kernel (PK), and ash from boiler furnaces. The high moisture content of EFBs prevents their immediate use as solid fuel. At most of the small-scale mills, the EFB are heaped and left to undergo decomposition. Some small-scale mills dry and use EFBs and palm press fibers as solid fuel for boiling the palm fruits as reported also by Gyamfi [24]. At the small-scale mills, palm kernels are mostly sold to palm kernel processors which are used to produce palm kernel oils.

4.5.2 Smoke

Smoke is generated from the boiling activities or open burning of EFBs. The smoke hangs over the mills causing discomfort to mill workers as noted by MASDAR [11]. The community members who reside close to the mills are also affected by the smoke. The smoke is mostly generated within the breathing zone of the mill workers which could potentially affect the health of the mill workers. In the study area, small-scale mills do not have in place measures and appropriate technology to control or manage smoke produced from their activities. In Elele, Nigeria, Ohimain and Izah [42] measured elevated concentrations of carbon monoxide, sulfur dioxide, nitrogen dioxide, volatile organic compounds, and suspended particulate matter at small-scale palm oil processing mills with most of the parameters above the Nigerian Ambient Air Quality standards. Diesel exhaust fumes from digesters contribute significantly to combustion-derived particulate matter air pollution [42].

4.5.3 Noise pollution

Mechanical digesters used by the mills produce noise. There is no technology in place to control the noise generated by the machinery used for processing. Application of noise-reduction technologies at small-scale processing mills in other study areas has not been reported in scientific literature. Moreover, the level of noise produced by the mechanical equipment used by small-scale mills in Ghana has not been investigated. In Nigeria, noise levels generated at small-scale mills were within permissible limits of 90 dB [43]. At the large mills in Ghana (such as Twifo Oil Palm Plantation), noise is minimized by installation of silencers to exhaust and rubber-lining ducts and cyclones within the plant controlling noise levels.

4.5.4 Odor nuisance

The odor at the small-scale processing mills studied is associated with rotten fruits, decomposing EFB and POME. Unpleasant odor pervades the mills and downwind of the POME and EFB disposal sites.

5. Implications of findings for policy and practice

The characteristics of the different wastewater streams and the current waste management practices at the small-scale mills in Ghana suggest the need to adopt appropriate and sustainable management practices.

5.1 Enforcement of environmental regulations

Wastewater is currently disposed on the bare ground without any form of treatment. Considering the characteristics and wastewater disposal practices, particular attention should be paid to the small-scale processing mills which dominate the palm oil production sector. In terms of policy, Regulation 1 of the Environmental Assessment Regulations, 1999 (LI 1652) [44] requires specific undertakings including oil and fats processing to register with and obtain environmental permit from the Ghana EPA prior to the commencement of the undertaking. In addition, existing undertakings, where EPA considers to have or is likely to have adverse effect on the environment or public health, are required to register with and obtain environmental permit in respect of the undertaking. Therefore, palm oil processing mills (including small-scale mills) are required to register with and obtain an environmental permit. However, small-scale processing mills belong to the informal sector where compliance to legal requirements is relatively weaker [22, 23]. The Ghana EPA, which is responsible for ensuring environmental compliance in Ghana, should extend enforcement of the Ghana Environmental Protection Requirements for Effluent Discharge to the small-scale (cottage) industries to ensure compliance. The government of Ghana, acting through the relevant agencies and the Artisanal Palm Oil Millers and Outgrowers Association, should provide technical support on sustainable waste management to the small-scale processing mills.

5.2 Selection of appropriate management solutions

Many technologies have been tested and applied to successfully treat palm oil mill wastewater mostly in Asia. Detailed description of different treatment methods can be found in the works by Liew, Kassim [45], Iskandar, Baharum [46] and Ohimain and Izah [47]. However, the selection of management solutions particularly for resource constrained environments such as what pertains in small towns and villages in Ghana where small-scale mills are located, must follow the principle of 'appropriate' technology. More importantly, the solution selected must lead to the recovery of valuable resources for beneficial use in the production process following the principles of circular economy.

5.2.1 Biogas production

The high BOD and appreciable concentration of nutrients (total nitrogen, phosphorus and potassium) and solids suggest the presence of considerable amount of organics which could serve as nutrients for microbial community in anaerobic digesters. Quah and Gillies [48] reported that anaerobic digestion of $1m^3$ of POME could generate $28m^3$ of biogas with 65% methane content. For small-scale palm oil mills in Ghana, the wastewater generated from the processing of one liter of crude palm oil could produce about 16–53 liters of biogas with 10.4–34.4 liters of methane content. Implementation of technologies to generate green energy would reduce the dependence on smoke-producing fuel wood which affects the health of the mill workers. Moreover, tapping the biogas for beneficial use would reduce the release of greenhouse gases into the environment.

5.2.2 Solid fuel production

Conversion of agricultural waste products into solid fuel has attracted attention and research. Empty fruit bunches, palm pressed fiber and sludge from palm oil mill wastewater are potential products for use as fuel. As has already been mentioned, limited quantities of EFB are dried and used as fuel by the small-scale mills. The suspended solids which contain solids and oils could be dried and used as solid fuel in the processing operations. The presence of unrecovered oil in palm pressed fiber is reported to enhance their combustibility and use in starting fires at the palm oil processing mills [49]. The potential of drying palm oil mill sludge and empty fruit bunch fiber for use as solid fuel has been reported by Awere, Bonoli [50]. Research must be directed at exploring different ways of converting the solid waste products into solid fuel which could be utilized in the production process or sold out to other industries.

5.2.3 Co-composting

Composting is the decomposition of organic residues into manure using a consortium of microorganisms (bacteria, actinomycetes and fungi) in a controlled environment. The high organic solids and appreciable nutrients content of POME [33, 47, 51] makes them potential substrates for compost production. In composting, wet substrates such as POME, low moisture bulking agents are required [52, 53]. POME may therefore be co-composted with bulking agents such empty palm fruit bunches and sawdust. Co-composting of POME with empty fruit bunches or saw dust has shown considerable success both at the laboratory and field scale. At a field-scale, Baharuddin, Wakisaka [54] co-composted partially treated POME from anaerobic pond with shredded empty fruit bunches (ratio of 1:3) over a 60-day period. The characteristics of the final compost showed considerable amounts of nutrients (carbon, nitrogen, phosphorus, potassium, calcium, magnesium, sulfur, and iron), trace amounts of manganese, zinc, and copper but very low levels of heavy metals. In a related study, palm oil mill sludge was co-composted with sawdust (1.86:1) over a 90-day period [55]. Through a pot experiment, the compost improved the growth of pseudostems of Cymbopogon citratus cultivated in a sandy soil.

Co-composting of POME significantly reduces the emission of greenhouse gases due to the aerobic decomposition process employed [56, 57]. The favorable climatic conditions of Ghana could enhance the compost production. The filtrate from the composting station could be assessed for their potential as liquid fertilizer.

5.2.4 Vermi-composting

An alternative to the conventional composting is vermi-composting which uses earthworms. Vermi-composting has been found to exhibit a higher rate of organic degradation and produce nutrient-rich compost with finer texture [58]. The composting period could be 50% of the time required by conventional composting systems. Composting of POME using earthworms has shown a great potential. Syirat, Ibrahim [59] used epigeic earthworms (Eudrillus eugeniae) to decompose POME sludge in a closed system within 60 days. They obtained a compost of high nutrient content compared with compost produced from EFB-POME sludge and mesocarp fiber-POME sludge. Similarly, Rupani, Embrandiri [60] used Lumbricus rubellus for vermi-composting POME-palm pressed fiber (1:1) over 30 days. The resulting compost showed significant improvement in nitrogen, phosphorus, and potassium content with 75% vermi-compost extract enhancing germination of mung bean. In another study, various compositions of empty fruit bunches and POME solid were vermi-composted using Eisenia fetida earthworms for 84 days [61]. In their study, a significant increase in total Kjeldhal nitrogen (0.4–1.7 mg/kg), total phosphorus (0.2–1.4 mg/kg) and total potassium (0.06–0.5 mg/kg) was recorded for all vermi-compost with the highest increase recorded for 1:1 EFB-POME solid combination. Vermi-composting produces two (2) important end products: manure/compost and earthworm biomass. The latter could be processed into protein source and sold to poultry and fish farmers [62].

6. Conclusion

The mean characteristics of wastewater produced during the peak season were generally higher than the lean season except for pH and solids (total and suspended). Irrespective of the production season, the wastewater was characterized by slowly biodegradable organic matter (COD: BOD_5 = 2.5–2.6). Wastewater from clarification had higher solids and nutrient content but lower oxygen-consuming compounds compared with wastewater from boiling. The current practice of disposing raw wastewater into the natural environment by the small-scale processing mills is negatively affecting the environment. Based on the characteristics of the wastewater and the tropical climatic conditions in Ghana, appropriate technologies that generate beneficial by-products such as biogas, compost or solid fuel must be explored. Enforcement of environmental regulations by the Ghana EPA should be extended to the small-scale (cottage) industries to ensure adoption of appropriate wastewater management technologies. Additional studies are needed in other palm oil production regions of Ghana to generate national-level data. This will guide the development of a compendium of wastewater treatment technologies applicable to small-scale processing mills in Ghana.

Conflict of interest

The authors have no conflicts of interest to declare that are relevant to the content of this article.

Author details

Eric Awere[1,2]*, Alessandra Bonoli[2], Peter Appiah Obeng[3], Sara Pennellini[2], Sara Bottausci[2], William Kwaasi Amanor[1] and Emmanuel Kekeli Akuaku[1]

1 Department of Civil Engineering, Cape Coast Technical University, Ghana

2 DICAM Department, University of Bologna, Bologna, Italy

3 Department of Water and Sanitation, University of Cape Coast, Cape Coast, Ghana

*Address all correspondence to: eric.awere@cctu.edu.gh

References

[1] FAOSTAT. Production Statistics - Crops, Crops Processed. In: Organization FaA, editor. FAOSTAT, Paris, 2022.

[2] Angelucci F. Analysis of Incentives and Disincentives for Palm Oil in Ghana. Rome: Technical Notes Series, MAFAP, FAO; 2013

[3] Opoku J, Asante F. Palm Oil Production in Ghana, Final Report on the Status of the Oil Palm Industry in Ghana. Accra: German Technical Co-operation (GTZ); 2008

[4] Yawson GK. Overview of the oil palm industry in Ghana. 2015. Available from: https://inclusivevcc.files.wordpress.com/2015/09/overview-of-ghanas-oil-palm-industry-by-george-kojo-yawson1.pdf

[5] GSS, GHS, ICF Macro. Demographic and Health Survey 2008. Accra, Ghana: GSS, GHS and ICF Macro; 2009

[6] IndexMundi. Ghana palm oil production by year 2022. Available from: https://www.indexmundi.com/agriculture/?country=gh&commodity=palm-oil&graph=production

[7] Commodafrica. Palm oil: The boomerang effect of the European decision Paris: Commodafrica. 2018. Available from: http://www.commodafrica.com/sites/commodafrica.com/files/dossiers-mois/huile_de_palmev5-uk.pdf

[8] Rhebergen T, Fairhurst T, Zingore S, Fisher M, Oberthür T, Whitbread A. Climate, soil and land-use based land suitability evaluation for oil palm production in Ghana. European Journal of Agronomy. 2016;**81**:1-14

[9] TrendEconomy. Annual International Trade Statistics by Country (HS02). Ghana Palm Oil Imports and Exports, 2006-2019 [Internet]. 2021. Available from: https://trendeconomy.com/data/h2/Ghana/1511. [Accessed: March 3, 2021]

[10] Poku K. Small-scale palm oil processing in Africa. Rome: Food & Agriculture Organization of the United Nations; 2002

[11] MASDAR. Master Plan Study on the Oil Palm Industry in Ghana: Final Report. Hampshire, UK: MASDAR House; 2011

[12] Hassan MA, Njeshu G, Raji A, Zhengwuvi L, Salisu J. Small-scale palm oil processing in west and Central Africa: Development and challenges. Journal of Applied Sciences & Environmental Sustainability. 2016;**2**(5):102-114

[13] Kajisa K, Maredia MK, Boughton D. Transformation Versus Stagnation in the Oil Palm Industry: A Comparison between Malaysia and Nigeria. Michigan: Michigan State University, Department of Agricultural, Food, and Resource Economics; 1997

[14] Uckert G, Hoffmann H, Graef F, Grundmann P, Sieber S. Increase without spatial extension: Productivity in small-scale palm oil production in Africa—The case of Kigoma, Tanzania. Regional Environmental Change. 2015;**15**(7):1229-1241

[15] Osei-Amponsah C, Visser L, Adjei-Nsiah S, Struik P, Sakyi-Dawson O, Stomph T. Processing practices of small-scale palm oil producers in the Kwaebibirem District, Ghana: A diagnostic study. NJAS-Wageningen Journal of Life Sciences. 2012;**60**:49-56

[16] Okwute LO, Isu NR. The environmental impact of palm oil mill effluent (pome) on some physico-chemical parameters and total aerobic bioload of soil at a dump site in Anyigba, Kogi state, Nigeria. African Journal of Agricultural Research. 2007;**2**(12):656-662

[17] APHA, AWWA, WEF. Standard Methods for the Examination of Water and Wastewater. 23rd ed. Washington, DC: American Public Health Association; 2017

[18] Adjei-Nsiah S, Zu A, Nimoh F. Technological and financial assessment of small scale palm oil production in Kwaebibrem district, Ghana. Journal of Agricultural Science. 2012;**4**(7):111-120

[19] Nkongho RN, Nchanji Y, Tataw O, Levang P. Less oil but more money! Artisanal palm oil milling in Cameroon. African Journal of Agricultural Research. 2014;**9**(20):1586-1596

[20] Taiwo K, Owolarafe O, Sanni L, Jeje J, Adeloye K, Ajibola O. Technological assessment of palm oil production in Osun and Ondo states of Nigeria. Technovation. 2000;**20**(4):215-223

[21] Anyaoha KE, Sakrabani R, Patchigolla K, Mouazen AM. Evaluating oil palm fresh fruit bunch processing in Nigeria. Waste Management Research. 2018;**36**(3):236-246

[22] Osei-Boateng C, Ampratwum E. The Informal Sector of Ghana. Accra: Friedrich Ebert Stiftung; 2011

[23] Ministry of Employment and Labour Relations. Ghana National Employment Policy. Accra: Ministry of Employment and Labour Relations; 2014

[24] Gyamfi I. Assessing environmental and social impacts of the oil palm industry in Ghana: A project synthesis. African Journal of Agricultural Research. 2017;**12**(8):632-641

[25] GSA. Environmental Protection - Requirements for Effluent Discharge. Accra, Ghana: Ghana Standard Authority; 2019

[26] Iwuagwu JO, Ugwuanyi JO. Treatment and valorization of palm oil mill effluent through production of food grade yeast biomass. Journal of Waste Management. 2014;**2014**(439071):7

[27] Wood B, Pillai K, Rajaratnam J. Palm oil mill effluent disposal on land. Agricultural Wastes. 1979;**1**(2):103-127

[28] Henze M, van Loosdrecht MCM, Ekama GA, Brdjanovic D. Biological Wastewater Treatment. London: IWA Publishing; 2008. p. 528

[29] Cisterna-Osorio P, Arancibia-Avila P. Comparison of biodegradation of fats and oils by activated sludge on experimental and real scales. Water. 2019;**11**(6):1286

[30] Salmiati Y, Salim MR, Ujang Z, Olsson G. COD fractionation of palm oil mill effluent: Typical treatment, biodegradability and modelling. Sustainable Environment Research. 2010;**20**(6):353-359

[31] Rupani PF, Singh RP, Ibrahim MH, Esa N. Review of current palm oil mill effluent (POME) treatment methods: Vermicomposting as a sustainable practice. World Applied Sciences Journal. 2010;**11**(1):70-81

[32] Likeng-Li-Ngue BC, Ntsomboh-Ntsefong G, Ngando-Ebongue GF, Ngalle-Bille H, Nyouma A, Bell JM. A review of main factors affecting palm oil acidity within the smallholder oil palm (Elaeis

guineensis Jacq.) sector in Cameroon. African Journal of Food Science. 2017;**11**(9):296-301

[33] Ahmad AL, Ismail S, Bhatia S. Water recycling from palm oil mill effluent (POME) using membrane technology. Desalination. 2003;**157**(1-3):87-95

[34] Khalid A, Mustafa WW. External benefits of environmental regulation: Resource recovery and the utilisation of effluents. Environmentalist. 1992;**12**(4):277-285

[35] Saari GN, Wang Z, Brooks BW. Revisiting inland hypoxia: Diverse exceedances of dissolved oxygen thresholds for freshwater aquatic life. Environmental Science and Pollution Research. 2018;**25**(4):3139-3150

[36] Von Sperling M. Wastewater Characteristics, Treatment and Disposal. London: IWA Publishing; 2007

[37] Bi C-h, Min M, Nie Y, Xie Q-L, Lu Q, Deng X-Y, et al. Process development for scum to biodiesel conversion. Bioresource Technology. 2015;**185**:185-193

[38] Ahmad A, Ghufran R. Review on industrial wastewater energy sources and carbon emission reduction: Towards a clean production. International Journal of Sustainable Engineering. 2019;**12**(1):47-57

[39] Loh SK, Lai ME, Ngatiman M, Lim WS, Choo YM, Zhang Z, et al. Zero discharge treatment technology of palm oil mill effluent. Journal of Oil Palm Research. 2013;**25**(3):273-281

[40] Tan YD, Lim JS. Feasibility of palm oil mill effluent elimination towards sustainable Malaysian palm oil industry. Renewable and Sustainable Energy Reviews. 2019;**111**:507-522

[41] Loh S, Nasrin A, Mohamad Azri S, Nurul Adela B, Muzzammil N. Biogas capture–a means of reducing greenhouse gas emissions from palm oil mill effluent. Oil Palm Bulletin. 2017;**75**:27-36

[42] Ohimain E, Izah S. Water minimization and optimization by small-scale palm oil mill in Niger Delta, Nigeria. Journal of Water Research. 2013;**135**:190-198

[43] Izah SC, Angaye TC, Ohimain EI. Environmental impacts of oil palm processing in Nigeria. Biotechnological Research. 2016;**2**(3):132-141

[44] Ministry of Environment Science and Technology. Environmental Assessment Regulation, 1999 (LI 1652). Accra, Ghana: Ministry of Environment, Science and Technology; 1999

[45] Liew WL, Kassim MA, Muda K, Loh SK, Affam AC. Conventional methods and emerging wastewater polishing technologies for palm oil mill effluent treatment: A review. Journal of Environmental Management. 2015;**149**:222-235

[46] Iskandar MJ, Baharum A, Anuar FH, Othaman R. Palm oil industry in South East Asia and the effluent treatment technology—A review. Environmental Technology Innovation. 2018;**9**:169-185

[47] Ohimain EI, Izah SC. A review of biogas production from palm oil mill effluents using different configurations of bioreactors. Renewable Sustainable Energy Reviews. 2017;**70**:242-253

[48] Quah S, Gillies D. Practical experience in production and use of biogas. In: National Workshop on Oil Palm by-Product Utilization Session C: Biogas. Kuala Lumpur, Malaysia, December 14-15: Palm Oil Research Institute of Malaysia; 1983

[49] Heuzé V, Tran G, Sauvant D. Palm press fibre: Feedipedia, a programme by INRA, CIRAD, AFZ and FAO. 2015. Available from: https://www.feedipedia.org/node/15392. [Accessed: May 11, 2015].

[50] Awere E, Bonoli A, Obeng PA. Solids-liquid separation and solar drying of palm oil mill wastewater sludge: Potential for sludge reuse. Case Studies in Chemical and Environmental Engineering. 2020;**2**:100057

[51] Wang J, Mahmood Q, Qiu J-P, Li Y-S, Chang Y-S, Chi L-N, et al. Zero discharge performance of an industrial pilot-scale plant treating palm oil mill effluent. BioMed Research International. 2015;**2015**:9

[52] Imbeah M. Composting piggery waste: A review. Bioresource Technology. 1998;**63**(3):197-203

[53] Gea T, Barrena R, Artola A, Sánchez A. Optimal bulking agent particle size and usage for heat retention and disinfection in domestic wastewater sludge composting. Waste Management. 2007;**27**(9):1108-1116

[54] Baharuddin AS, Wakisaka M, Shirai Y, Abd-Aziz S, Abdul R, Hassan M. Co-composting of empty fruit bunches and partially treated palm oil mill effluents in pilot scale. International Journal of Agricultural Research. 2009;**4**(2):69-78

[55] Zahrim AY, Rakmi AR, Kalil MS. Sludge composting: A case study on palm oil mill sludge (POMS). ASEAN Journal of Chemical Engineering. 2007;**7**(1&2):102-107

[56] Hasanudin U, Haryanto A. Palm oil mill effluent recycling system for sustainable palm oil industries. Asian Journal of Environmental Technology. 2018;**2**(1):52-62

[57] Barik D. Chapter 3 - energy extraction from toxic waste originating from food processing industries. In: Barik D, editor. Energy from Toxic Organic Waste for Heat and Power Generation. Duxford, UK: Woodhead Publishing; 2019. pp. 17-42

[58] Lee ZS, Chin SY, Lim JW, Witoon T, Cheng CK. Treatment technologies of palm oil mill effluent (POME) and olive mill wastewater (OMW): A brief review. Environmental Technology & Innovation. 2019;**15**:100377

[59] Syirat ZB, Ibrahim MH, Astimar AA, Hayawin ZN. Changes in characteristics and physicochemical through vermicomposting of pome sludge by Epigeic Earthworm E. eugeniae. Advanced Materials Research. 2014;**970**:304-307

[60] Rupani PF, Embrandiri A, Ibrahim MH, Shahadat M, Hansen SB, Mansor NNA. Bioremediation of palm industry wastes using vermicomposting technology: Its environmental application as green fertilizer. 3. Biotech. 2017;**7**(3):155

[61] Nahrul Hayawin Z, Astimar AA, Anis M, Ibrahim MH, Khalil HPSA, Ibrahim Z. Vermicomposting of empty fruit bunch with addition of solid palm oil mill effluent. Journal of Oil Palm Research. 2012;**24**:1542-1549

[62] Parolini M, Ganzaroli A, Bacenetti J. Earthworm as an alternative protein source in poultry and fish farming: Current applications and future perspectives. Science of the Total Environment. 2020;**734**:139460

Chapter 6

Integrated Pest Management (IPM) in Oil Palm, *Elaeis guineensis* Jacq.

Rajasekhar Pinnamaneni and Kalidas Potineni

Abstract

The edible oil of *Elaeis guineensis* Jacq., oil palm, is crucial in filling the demand gap and meet the growing need for edible oil worldwide. Although all precautions have been taken to minimize the introduction of pest populations along with seed sprouts from importing countries, some pests are still found to invade crops and cause production losses. Most of these populations have been found to come from other Arecaceae palms such as coconut, palmyrah and betel nut that may be commonly found around oil palm fields. It has been estimated that the above pests reduced oil palm yield by 20–30%, persisted for several years after attack, depending on cultivation methods, and returned to previous yield levels within a few years of attack. The minor pests of coconut, palmyrah, and maize, psychid and slug caterpillar were discovered to be very invasive on oil palm, resulting in output losses of up to 50%. The presence of favorable conditions such as low temperature and high humidity within oil palm plantations may possibly be the reason for migration. The production losses caused by these migratory pests affect the sustainability of the produce and thus agriculture, so it is important to apply the good management practices.

Keywords: oil palm, pollinating weevil, rhinoceros beetle, caterpillars, integrated pest management

1. Introduction

Oil palm (*Elaeis guineensis* Jacq.), is a rich source of edible oil and is a perennial crop cultivated in large areas to beat the edible oil shortage. Upon cultivation, a farmer can draw the yield for 25–30 years, stabilising his economy over its other oil seed crops. Oil palm is cultivated in tropical areas of Asia, Africa, and South America. The productivity of the crop is challenged by the availability of water and nutrient stress, abiotic stress like drought, biotic stresses like pests and diseases, etc. As oil palm requires nearly 300 litres of water per day, irrigation should be continuous at regular intervals, therefore, the micro-climate so formed with high humidity and cold makes pleasant conditions for the event of pests and diseases. The age of the palms will dictate the incidence of pests. The pest infestation from foreign sources may be due to the strict quarantine measures being followed at various ports important for seed sprouts. The sole chance for the pest outbreak is that the migration of pests from other crops grown in the nearby locations of the oil palm plantations is because of the availability of food material continuously. The perennial nature of palms and the monocropping system as practiced in many locations provide ample opportunities for the buildup of the pest. The spread of the problems is slow in new areas. Of the insect pests, the most important is the rhinoceros beetle and defoliators, causing heavy yield losses. The insect pests which are reported as minor and secondary pests on other crops got the pest status as the damage was noticed in both nursery and field palms of oil palm. Oil palm, as it is a perennial crop, is gorgeous to several pests such as the defoliators (leaf-eating caterpillars) such as bagworms, nettle, and hairy caterpillars feed on the palm fonds, causing damage by defoliating the oil palm tree thereby resulting in yield loss because of the reduction of photosynthetic activity and fruit production. High population levels can result in the whole skeletonization and death of the fronds. Damage of 50% will cause a yield decline of around 43% over the following 2 years. Even lower damage like 10–13% also can cause an analogous loss [1]. Natural enemies including predatory or parasitic insects and diseases caused by viruses and fungi, caterpillars are effectively kept below the economic damage threshold under normal conditions. Heavy pest attack is usually the results of a breakdown within the balance of nature. Generalist predators might not totally feed on the oil palm caterpillars and instead take advantage of other insects available within the ecosystem. In search of hosts, dust under dry conditions interferes with predators and parasites. The parasitoids number may be reduced which are commonly attacked by hyperparasitoids. Outbreaks of the caterpillars are sporadic and localised, thereby; parasites and predators do not fully control the caterpillar populations' altogether years and locations. A monitoring and closed-circuit television for oil palm is in practice for several years. By monitoring a pestilence, the world within which damage is happening is delineated [2]. Chemical intervention is merely used when populations reach threatening levels by injecting the trunk with a systemic insecticide that is translocated within the sap and carried into the leaf tissue. This implies that only the leaf-feeding caterpillars are killed, but not their natural enemies. Overall insecticide use is low, with no quite 5% of the whole area of oil palms receiving application in anyone year. Insecticide application averages about once in an exceedingly planting generation (around 25 years). In many instances, smallholders do not regularly manage the caterpillar populations with trunk injections and high uncontrolled outbreaks occur [3]. Chemical control typically takes place too late to prevent large production losses due to complex application techniques, subpar monitoring mechanisms, and therefore the challenging environment. Chemical application is also expensive and bad for the environment. There's enormous potential to boost the present pest management practices, and a number of other biological control agents may well be utilised in integrated pest management (IPM) systems [4]. Agronomic practices directed toward developing biodiversity within the oil palm cropping system, and improved pest monitoring and surveying could even be components of this IPM. The practice of Integrated Pest Management (IPM) against several pests and diseases (P&D) of oil palm includes holistic approaches designed for a P&D control program to cut back pest populations below the brink level with minimal environmental impact [5].

2. Pollinating Weevil, *Elaedobius kamerunicus*

2The pollinating weevil, *Elaedobius kamerunicus* (Coleoptera: Curculionidae) has been known to be the foremost efficient insect pollinator of oil palm and has successfully improved the pollination and increased the yield. Its introduction has greatly reduced the requirement for assisted pollination. *Elaeidobius kamerunicus* was introduced into Malaysia during the late 1980s to spice up the assembly of oil palm fruit bunches. Almost 40 years since the introduction of *E. kamerunicus*, significant improvements are witnessed within the increase of yield of oil palm. Nevertheless, the present concern within the oil palm sector is regarding the decreasing of fruit sets that will be plugged by *E. kamerunicus* [6]. Through their subsequent visits to the female inflorescences, when the stigmas are receptive, the female flower emits short pulses of an analogous but sharper and more penetrating odour that attracts Elaeidobius species apart from the male flowers and the pollen grains. The weevils chew the anther filaments of opened male flowers, during anthesis when a robust aniseed-like scent is emitted; they crawl or move about on the spikelets [7]. When the weevils crawl over the male inflorescences an outsized number of pollen grains are dispersed which are carried by wind [8]. The weevils enter the female inflorescence but quickly leave after finding no food there, returning to the male flowers. When *Elaeidobius* species crawl around the female inflorescence, pollen is discharged, which causes them to become covered in it. Over 5000 beetles are thought to visit each female inflorescence during receptivity, and each one can carry up to 600 pollen grains. The development of the larvae occurs on tissue that has served its role and has no utility for the palm because oviposition occurs after anthesis, hence *Elaeidobius* species do not significantly harm the palm [9]. The most ideal insect for introduction into Malaysia and other regions with poor oil palm pollination is *E. kamerunicus*. *E. kamerunicus*, one of the many species of this genus investigated in Cameroon, was the most prevalent in the country's coastal regions throughout both the wet and dry seasons, transported more pollen than other species, and had a respectable ability to search (**Figure 1**) [10].

The weevils are quite useful, and man has introduced them to palm farms to use them for pollinating those trees. In regions where palms and weevils were not native, hand pollination was used, which was exceedingly expensive for the growers. The inadequate pollination has been a significant issue in these nations. In addition to the slow pace of fruit establishment, inadequate pollination can occasionally cause bunch failure [11].

The Tenera palm variety demonstrated larger yield improvement as a result of *E. kamerunicus* introduction to Malaysia than the Dura variety. Larger, heavier, and more compact bunches were assembled as a result of weevil pollination, which also increased the oil to bunch ratio from under 19 to 23–25%, especially on trees that were 4–10 years old. *Thrips hawaiiensis*, an older, less effective pollinator, was not ostensibly replaced by *E. kamerunicus*. In terms of pollinating oil palms, the weevil population is crucial. Weevil populations have been found to be reduced by a number of

Figure 1.
Pollinating Weevil, Elaeidobius kamerunicus. *(A) Female inflorescence, (B) male inflorescence, (C) pollinating Weevil,* Elaeidobius kamerunicus, *(D) pollinating weevils on male inflorescence, (E) weevil at a spiklet of oil palm male flower.*

factors, including climate, pesticides, interactions with other insects in the area, and male inflorescence [12]. The pollinator force of the weevil was sustained at a spread between 3095.2 and 19126.1 weevils per ha. The mean of weevils per spikelet shows that the range of weevils was between 13.51 and 54.06 per spikelet. There was no correlation between rainfall and population density of EK. However, a correlation was obtained between weevil density and therefore the number of anthesis female inflorescence of oil palm ($r = 0.938$, $p < 0.05$). Results of the t-test show that the 6-year-old oil palm stands had a significantly different population density than that of an 8-year-old oil palm stand. The data of this study should be useful as baseline data to analyse why there's such a large range of weevils per ha or spikelet [13].

The natural enemies of the pollinating weevil, *E. kamerunicus* are the parasitoid nematodes *Aphelenchoides bicaudatus* and *Cylindrocorpus inevectus* attacking during pupal stage [14]. The pupae were found to be severely infested with *A. bicaudatus* then were treated until nematode-free before being released [15]. The nematode *Elaeolenchus parthenonema* is harmful to the weevil [16], but the *Bacillus thuringiensis* products Lepcon-1, Bafog-1 (S), and Ecobac-1 (EC) are proven innocuous to the weevil [17].

In order to search out the impact of bio-agents together with chemical insecticides on the expansion and survival of the pollinating weevils of oil palm, the study was distributed. Newly emerging inflorescences in 24 palms were selected and tagged for applying pesticides and bio-agents. Conventional insecticides quinalphos (0.05%), monocrotophos (0.072%), lambda cyahalothrin (0.02%), and microbial agents namely *Metarhizium anisopliae* (6.4×10^5 spores/ml) and *Beauveria bassiana* (3.5×10^5 spores/ml) at normal concentrations were tested as treatments by applying on the inflorescence as a liquid spray. The concentrations of these selected chemical insecticides were proved lethal to the target pests of oil palm. The population count of the weevils (egg to adult stages) was recorded employing a sampling technique. Daily weather data was also recorded during the observation period to correlate the population fluctuation if any with the abiotic factors. Observations recorded on the weevil population showed significant results. Analysis of the obtained data was met out using the chi-square test. The chi-square test results clearly indicate that the difference within the weevil population in untreated and insecticide-treated palms is very significant and contrarywise in untreated and microbial agents viz. *Metarhizium anisopliae* and *Beauveria bassiana*. The chemical pesticide quinalphos had a major impact in reducing the weevil population whereas the microbial agents did not cause a major reduction. However, *Metarhizium anisopliae*, which may be a good microbial agent against many coleopteran pests, was observed to cause less impact on the pollinating weevils which are coleopterans. This means that the microbial agents are safer for pollinating weevils compared to the standard pesticide and hence, can safely be included within the oil palm pest management practices [18].

3. Pests of oil palm

Prior to field planting, oil palm is usually passed through single or double stage nursery system. Oil palm seedlings are maintained for 12–14 months in nursery and culled and planted within the field. Preventive measures such as insecticide application at frequent intervals protect the nurseries and are almost free from pest incidence. However, when within the neglected conditions, few pests are observed causing damage to the seedlings. A number of them are listed below (**Tables 1** and **2**).

Pests		Common name	Scientific name
Insects	Lepidoptera	Tussock caterpillar	*Dasychira mendosa* Hb.
	Lepidoptera	Psychid	*Metisa plana Walker*
	Lepidoptera	Leaf webworm	*Acria meyricki*
	Lepidoptera	Tobacco caterpillar	*Spodoptera litura* Fb.
	Hemiptera	Spindle bug	*Carvalhoia arecae* Miller
	Homoptera	Leaf hopper	*Proutista moesta* Westwood
	Homoptera	Aphids	*Cerataphis brasiliensis*
	Coleoptera	Cockchafer beetles (Root grub)	*Apogonia/Adoretus* spp.
Molluscan pests		Black slug	*Laevicaulis alte*
Vertebrate pests		Black rat	*Rattus rattus* Wroughtoni
		Wild boar	*Sus scrofa*

Table 1.
Pests of oil palm nursery.

Pests		Common name	Scientific name
Insects	Coleoptera	Rhinoceros beetle	*Oryctes rhinoceros* L.
	Lepidoptera	Tussock caterpillar	*Dasychira mendosa Hb.*
	Lepidoptera	Slug caterpillar	*Darna catenatus*
	Lepidoptera	Psychid	*Metisa plana Walker*
	Lepidoptera	Leaf webworm	*Acria meyricki*
	Hemiptera	Coccoids (scales and mealy bugs)	*Hemiberlesia lataniae*, *Chrysomphalus aonidum*, *Pinnapsis aspidistrae*, *Dysmicoccus brevipes*
	Isoptera	Termites	*Coptotermes curvignathus*
Vertebrates	Avian pests	Crows	*Convus splendens protegatus*; *Corvus macrorhynchus cuiminatus*
		Mynah	*Acridotheres tristis*
		Babbler	*Turdoides affinis affinis*
		Parrots	*Psitticula krameri manillensis*
	Mammalian pests	Black rat	*Ratus rattus wroughtoni*
		House rat	*Rattus rattus rufescens*
		Western Ghat squirrel	*Funambulus tristriatus*
		Procupines	*Hystrix indica*

Table 2.
Pests of oil palm plantations.

4. Insect pests

Insect pests are the most limiting factor for crop production in tropical Asia, among which Lepidopteran pests cause a major amount of injury. Oil yielding and vegetables are the foremost profitable crops and farmers everywhere feel the requirement to shield such high value crops from any style of damage caused by insect pests.

4.1 Lepidopteran pests

4.1.1 Tussock caterpillar: Dasychira mendosa *Hb. (Lymantridae)*

It is a polyphagous insect, which is mostly found on edible seeds, citrus, guava, banana, etc. Significant damage to nursery seedlings is due to the larvae which occasionally feed voraciously on the leaves. They're found to cause damage in oil palm plantations also [19]. This pest was observed in oil palm nurseries. The pest is found round the year with the peak incidence during June–July, with the onset of heavy rains [20]. Incidence is seen only in those nurseries which are overgrown and not lifted for transplantation at the proper time (**Figure 2**).

4.1.1.1 Biology and nature of injury

About 302.9 eggs are laid by a female moth in its lifetime within a period of about 5.5 days. After hatching, the larvae withstand 9–10 instars in 43.1 days. The

Figure 2.
Tussock caterpillar.

larvae are found defoliating the oil palm severely at the secondary nursery stage. Initially the leaves are scraped by the young larvae within the congregation and later disperse and begin feeding on the tender leaves severely. The complete life cycle from egg to adult is 65.1 days. Caterpillars possess dense tufts of hair on the body. They are capable of causing minor irritation and sometimes rash on the material body.

4.1.1.2 Management

Under the field conditions, tachinid flies parasitizes the larvae to 10.2% and pupae by are parasitized by *Brachymeria albotibialis* to 40.0%. The pest can managed with 1–2 sprays of 0.05% quinalphos. The larvae of *D. mendosa* are parasitized by a tachinid fly (Diptera: Tachinidae) and the pupae of *D. mendosa* are parasitized by *Brachymeria albotibialis* (Ashmead) (Hymenoptera: Chalcididae). The fly injects an egg into the caterpillar. The fly maggots burrow inside the host and feed from inside the body upon hatching. The affected caterpillar becomes sluggish reduces in size and fails to pupate and eventually dies. The mean parasitism is generally about 10.2% during the pest activity period. The parasitized pupa turns dark brown or black in colour and only one parasitoid individual emerges out per host pupa. Once the parasitoid emerged, the empty pupal case remained with a circular hole at the pinnacle region. The extent of parasitism under field conditions is often recorded as 40.0%. This information on biology, the character of the damage, seasonal activity, and natural enemies of *D. mendosa* can be used for planning and developing effective pest management strategies in oil palm nurseries.

4.1.2 Slug caterpillar Darna catenatus *Snellen, (Limacodidae)*

The pest was reported as a significant problem in both Malaysia and Indonesia where large hectares of oil palm was infested with it causing heavy defoliation [21]. The incidence of slug caterpillar was first reported on oil palm in 2002 was sporadic and erratic in very few plantations of West Godavari and Krishna districts of Andhra Pradesh, India. The pest was also observed feeding on the adjacent coconut plants but at low levels and doubtless migrated to the oil palm thanks to the provision of lush green leaves. However, it was shown that high summer temperatures had little effect on insect build-up and that a high ratio was a key element in natural suppression (**Figure 3**).

4.1.2.1 Biology and nature of harm

Every female lays between 250 and 350 eggs. On the abaxial surfaces of the more developed fronds, frequently close to the edges of leaflets, the eggs are placed in rows. These eggs will eventually hatch. The caterpillars have urticating spines and are green. Caterpillars in the first instar solely eat the epidermis, which results in translucent patches that resemble windows. Later-stage caterpillars eat from the lamina's margin toward the interior, leaving the midvein. The larva develops during a period of 3–7 weeks. To spin cocoons and pupate, caterpillars scurry way down to the tree trunk's base or amid herbaceous plants. The pupal stage is for 2–4 weeks. The destructive stage, caterpillars, are observed feeding on the leaf lamina, severely defoliating the leaf and leaving just the midribs. The lower whorl leaves have totally

Figure 3.
Slug caterpillar infecting oil palm.

dried due to the heavy incidence. Faecal droppings on the bottom level or cover and the sound of gnawing during a significant outbreak can both be used to gauge the pest's severity. The larvae are found to own setae on the dorsal side of the body causing irritation to handle. The presence of a bluish tinge on the dorsal side of the caterpillar is the conspicuous identification mark of the pest. Except for oil palm, the incidence was also observed in cocoa and maize that are grown within or adjacent to oil palm plantations. The caterpillars are characterised by their stinging spines which may cause a rash on contact with the skin. Young caterpillars scrape strips of the epidermis and as they become mature, generally commence feeding near the information of pinnae, leaving only the midrib [19]. The fronds are severely defoliated during a severe epidemic, leaving the midrib alone.

4.1.2.2 Management

a. At the beginning of the pest activity period, lower fronds with pest stages should be pruned and burned.

b. Natural suppression of the pest is observed in very few plantations thanks to virus infections. Virus infection to the caterpillars arresting the moulting process is observed in severely infested gardens.

c. Application of microorganism, *Beauveria bassiana* (10^{-1}) that caused white muscardine disease to the caterpillar proved effective but time taking compared to chemical insecticides.

d. Under natural conditions, an oversized number of parasitoids of Eulophidae, Chalcididae, Braconidae, Tachinidae, and Bombyliidae and predators of Hemiptera and Pentatomidae families regulate the host populations [22].

e. For the control, carbaryl 50% WP is advised to be sprayed at 0.1% [23].

f. The pest can be successfully controlled by two aerial applications of quinolphos 0.05% or lambda-cyhalothrin 0.05% spaced 15 days apart throughout the period of pest activity.

g. When the palms have reached their full height, stem injection with monocrotophos 25/100 ml of water per palm is also useful.

4.1.3 Bag worm, Metisa plana *(Psychidae)*

Bag worm, *Metista plana* is observed in moderate levels with quite six case worms per leaflet in Andhra Pradesh state all the year round. However in Karnataka the incidence is heavy during the monsoon and winter months. Cocoa (*Theobroma cacao*), coconut (*Cocos nucifera*), edible seed (*Areca catechu*) and areca palm (*Dypsis lutescens*) are observed as collateral hosts for the pest. There are nine different species of caseworms known to infest oil palm in India. *Metisa plana*, *Manatha albipes*, and *Crematopsyche pendula* were the most often seen species. In almost all the gardens, the pest is observed endemic with the presence of all the stages at any date of observation. Psychid incidence is observed during of July to March leaving the summer months with a percent incidence varying 0.39–8.8 in several palms. Young gardens of but 5 years recorded less incidence compared to middle aged ones. The fundamental cause of the higher prevalence compared to young gardens where such conditions are absent is the observed overlapping and intermixing of leaves of neighbouring palms, which prevents sunlight from penetrating into the older gardens. Unfavourable abiotic conditions, such as high temperatures during the pre-monsoon period, a delay in the monsoon, and heavy rains throughout the monsoon season, may be linked to the natural death of psychids that was seen over the summer and rainy period. Although the pest maintains congenial conditions suited to its growth and development within the bag by regulating the desired temperature and humidity, during this time of year it could not maintain dryness and through hot summers, it's unable to take care of the specified humidity resulting in mortality of the pest (**Figure 4**).

4.1.3.1 Biology and nature of harm

The pupal cocoons, which are hidden in sacks, contain 60–80 eggs laid by wingless female adults. The fecundity can occasionally be quite high. The egg cycle lasts 16 days. Before pupating, the larva typically needs 100–125 days. Just five larval instars are seen in males and seven instars in the case of females. The larvae and adults possess black pectinate antennae. Because the caterpillars mature, they turn within the bag, changing from a feeding position with their heads oriented toward the plant surface. It takes 26 days to reach the pupal stage. The primary instar larvae after hatching from eggs are naked with no bag. They start feeding on the mother's bag as soon as they hatch, eventually forming their own bag. Caterpillars live in a case while they are developing. Each species' case/bag has a specific form and outward

Figure 4.
Psychids feeding on oil palm.

appearance. The pupae are found within the luggage and are just plain cocoons. The males have wings and are able to fly.

The abaxial surfaces of the fronds are scarified by caterpillars in their early stages. The full leaf tissue is chewed by caterpillars in later instars, which also create holes and notches in the leaf tissue by feeding at the leaf margins. When bagworms feed, the surface develops holes and grooves as well as dry necrotic areas where the surface has been destroyed. Bagworms attack the center and older fronds of the palms, with younger fronds usually remaining free from damage. Damage by psychids is severe only the population is incredibly high. The yield of the palm suffers from gradual necrosis and ultimately skeletonization. Defoliation by the bug results in a loss of 3.88% of each palm's photosynthetic area.

4.1.3.2 Management

a. Regular cutting and burning of the severely damaged and dried leaves that contain insect stages reduces the population.

b. Three species of parasitoids namely *Goriphous bunoh* infesting pupal stages and *Brachymeria* spp. and *Dolichogenidea metesae* infesting larval stages of the pest are recorded in the majority of the plantations [24, 25]. The impact of parasitism on the pest population is observed more within the later stages of the pest. Brachymeria spp. is observed because the main parasitoid causes over 40% parasitism to larval stages. The typical percent parasitism is observed at 33.15% with maximum parasitization (65.23%) during the month of November while minimum (15.83%) during December.

c. Aerial spraying of lambda cyhalothrin 0.05% is typically advised in cases of severe infestation. Since immature larvae are more susceptible to pesticides, spraying should be timed to coincide with their most frequent occurrences. If the palms grow too tall and cannot be sprayed, systemic insecticides like monocrotophos or imidacloprid may be be applied via stem injection or root feeding. If sprayed correctly and irrigated, granular pesticides like phorate or carbofuran applied at a rate of 100–150 g per palm in a basin may also be beneficial.

4.1.4 Leaf web worm, Acria meyricki *(Depressaridae)*

The pest was first recorded during the winter months of 1995–1996 [26]. The occurrence was erratic for a decade and later confined to few gardens in alternate years. From 2005 onwards, it's become an everyday pest occurring each year in Krishna, East, and West Godavari districts of the state. In some regions where palm trees have grown to a certain height and where the leaves of nearby palm trees combine, the pest has become endemic. This has created an ideal environment for the insect's growth. In those orchards where the palms received more basin irrigation due to flood irrigation with more water than necessary, the infestation was made worse. The leaf webworm, *A. meyricki*, has been linked to yield losses of up to 34%. It was only occasionally and sporadically seen as a pest during the winter. The bug disappears as the temperature rises. Typically, the incidence is seen between October and April. It was discovered that the larval population had a substantial negative correlation with weather variables including maximum and lowest temperatures, and that the relationship between the mean temperature and ratio and rainfall was insignificant (**Figure 5**) [27, 28].

Figure 5.
Leaf web worm on oil palm.

4.1.4.1 Biology and nature of injury

About 62.5 eggs are laid by a female moth in clusters (in confined conditions). The time span is 4–6 days, with 4.7 days serving as the median. Egg hatchability is 95.6%, ranging from 92.8 to 100%. The larval stage has 6–7 instars, which it goes through in an incredibly long 20.7 days. The larva reaches the pre-pupal stage, which lasts 1 day, when it has reached maturity, stops feeding, shrinks in size, and ceases growing. Pupa stage duration is 5.8 days. A typical adult lives for 5.4 days. From egg to adult stage, the entire life span begins in 30–44 days [29]. The larval stage that remains inside and is active on the underside of the leaves is the caterpillar. The early instars scrape the leaves, and the later instars cause defoliation.

They first cause significant defoliation by nibbling on the elder leaves. The caterpillars go to the following top leaves once the lower leaves have completely been destroyed. Due of a bad infestation, the leaflets were dried out and gave off the appearance of being burned. When disturbed, the larvae dangle from silken threads and either go to nearby palm trees or are pulled back and pursue the same leaves. The infection can easily spread due to the intermixing of palm fronds in the garden. The larvae are discovered eating on cocoa, *Theobroma cocoa*, coconut, *Cocos nusifera* and decorative edible seed, *Areca catechu*, banana, and a few different kinds of grass in the gardens during a serious infestation. When oil palm and cocoa are intercropped, cocoa is frequently infested.

4.1.4.2 Management

a. At the beginning of the pest activity period, lower fronds with pest stages should be pruned and burned.

b. Under field conditions, two biocontrol agents, *Apanteles hyposidrae* Wilkinson (Hymenoptera: Ichneumonoidea: Braconidae) and *Elasmus brevicornis* Gahan, are found parasitizing larvae (Hymenoptera: Chalcidoidea: Eulophidae). Elasmid and braconid parasitism rates on larvae range from 21.41 to 36.58%, while *Brachymeria albotibialis* (Ashmead) (Hymenoptera: Chalcidoidea: Chalcididae) parasitizes pupa, the percent parasitism varies from 21.21 to 79.75.

c. The use of microbial organisms such *Beauveria bassiana*, *Metarhizium anisopliae*, and *Verticillium lecanii*, of which *Beauveria bassiana* effectively checks the pest population, is an effective method of pest management.

d. It has been shown to be efficient in suppressing the pest to use lambda-cyhalothrin or quinalphos 0.05 or 0.05% twice during the pest activity period at intervals of 15 days.

e. Injection of the stem with monocrotophos 25/100 ml of water per palm is additionally effective within the case of tall palms.

4.1.5 Tobacco caterpillar, Spodoptera litura *Fb. (Noctuidae)*

During the months of February and March, sporadic instances of the bug feeding on the oil palm nursery leaves are noted. This is particularly typical in nurseries that

Figure 6.
Life cycle of Tobacco caterpillar.

are built close to tobacco or corn fields. After harvesting the nearby corn fields, the insect may migrate to the oil palm plantations (**Figure 6**).

4.1.5.1 Nature and symptoms of damage

The destructive signs include defoliation of young leaves and feeding symptoms on the primordial region.

4.1.5.2 Management

With the application of contact pesticides like quinalphos (0.05%), the pest can be controlled.

4.1.6 Shoot borer: Sesamia inferens *walker (Noctuidae)*

All of the southern states of India, including Andhra Pradesh, Karnataka, and Kerala, have primary and secondary nurseries with oil palm seedlings where the shoot borer is present (**Figure** 7).

4.1.6.1 Nature and symptoms of damage

Caterpillars enter the stem by the spindle leaf rachis, eat on the meristematic tissues, which result in symptoms like a dead heart and undersized leaves, and therefore hinder the growth. Pink caterpillars develop inside the rachis of the leaf. It has been noted that severe infestation kills secondary nursery plants of the oil palm,

Figure 7.
Life cycle of shoot borer.

necessitating management actions. Nurseries that are poorly run have been proven to be more vulnerable to a shoot borer infestation.

4.1.6.2 Management

A bimonthly application of Carbaryl 50% WP 0.01% will reduce the occurrence of shoot borer [30].

4.2 Coleopteran pests

4.2.1 Rhinoceros beetle, Oryctes rhinoceros *L. (Scarabaeidae)*

It is a standard pest of the many palms including coconut, oil palm, edible seed and palmyra palms all through the states of India. It became a major pest in all the Indian states that grow oil palm [31]. It's found throughout South-East Asia and plenty of oil palm-growing countries. Pest incidence is found throughout the year but its incidence where adult emergence is at its peak during South-West Monsoon (June to September). This means that pest emergence synchronises with the monsoon showers. Infestation is severe in plantations where field hygiene and sanitation are neglected. Palmyrah palm (*Borasses flabellifer*), coconut, arecanut are collateral hosts of this pest (**Figure 8**) [24, 32, 33].

This Rhonoceros beetle was found migrated from other palms such as coconut and palmyra during the initial periods of crop establishment. But within the recent period, it's found to reject the oil palm. This is often particularly seen when coconut plants are adjacent to these palms. The presence of more lignin at the place of feeding (leaf petiole) in oil palm compared to leaf tips within the case of other Arecaceae palms is that the prime reason for low pest incidence of the pest [34]. This also indicates the pest preference for a specific place of the crop. Costa Rican material, Deli X Ghana is found to be the smallest amount at risk of scarabaeid beetle attack followed by Deli X Nigerian cross. The Malaysian variety Gutherie is found more vulnerable to the beetle followed by Palode material [27].

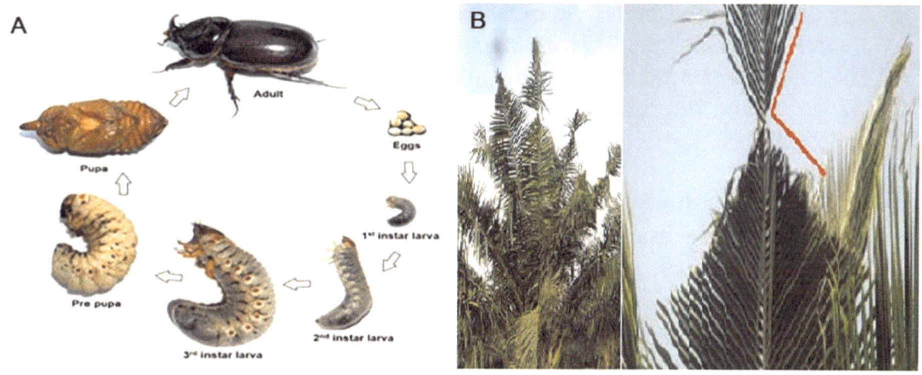

Figure 8.
A. Life cycle of Rhinoceros Beetle; B. Symptoms of Rhinoceros Beetle infestation on oil palm.

4.2.1.1 Biology and nature of damage

The oval, white eggs are placed at a depth of 5–10 cm in the surface of decomposing organic waste. The earliest stages of the beetle typically occur in manure pits, compost piles, rotting palm logs and stumps, decomposing organic materials like animal dung, and manure pits. Additionally, the oil palm leaf axils, decaying inflorescences, and mounds of mesocarp on the plantation are all places where the beetles can breed [35, 36]. A female lays between 100 and 150 eggs, which take 8–18 days to hatch. Once they do, the grubs begin to feed on the decomposing materials. The larvae endure three instars and reach maturity in 100–180 days depending on the conditions. The beetle pupates in a deep chamber at a depth of around 30 cm, and it emerges after 10–25 days. They remain in the pupal stage for another 10–20 days. After 20–60 days, they begin to lay eggs. In the dark hours, beetles are busy and drawn to sources of light. A grownup can live for more than 200 days. Typically, one generation is finished each year. When the spear cluster is closed, adult beetles penetrate into the palms at the base to eat the sap and delicate sections of the leaves. The beetles enter the spear cluster's inner petiole through its outermost petiole, causing a hole that will remain there forever. The frequent symptoms include a hole in the petiole and a wedge-shaped gap in the leaf profile. Compared to adult palms, young palms show much more severe damage near the bottom of the spears. Expanded fronds may break off or become truncated, or the damaged spindle may collapse. Even before anthesis, while the inflorescences are still inside the spathe, adult rhinoceros beetles have been observed digging and devouring the male and female inflorescences [37]. Beetles can be identified by their entry holes because they leave behind chewed-up fibrous fibres [19]. Because of the infiltration of fungi and bacteria through the injuries the insect caused to the palm's internal organs, secondary rotting of the bud is typically observed. The red palm weevil's functional birthing sites are wounds formed on petioles and female inflorescences.

4.2.1.2 Management

An integrated pest management approach by incorporating mechanical, sanitation, chemical, and biological aspects is required to combat the pest menace. Identifying all potential pest breeding locations and keeping an eye on the beetle population on the palm's crown are crucial parts of pest management technology.

a. A hooked, pointed metal rod must be used to extricate the insects from the crowns of immature palm trees because they dig there deeply (beetle hook). The leaf axils around the injured spindle or leaf are to be filled with a mixture of Mancozeb and sterilised fine sand at a ratio of 3 g:1 kg once the beetle has been removed.

b. Leaf axil filling should be done as a preventative measure to protect young palm trees from beetle attack. During April–May, September–October, and December–January, a mixture of Sevidol 8 G (25 g) + fine sand (200 g) is additionally packed into the innermost 2–3 leaf axils of each palm. Care should be used when using the sand, though, as it may contain organisms that reproduce to cause disease.

c. The plantation must be cleared of any potential breeding locations. Carbaryl 50% WP 0.01% is to be sprayed on any breeding grounds that cannot be eradicated or destroyed.

d. Due to the oil palm's monthly production of two leaves, the granules given to the crown section have proven ineffectual unless they are removed and applied to a fresh spindle each month. It is difficult and time-consuming since the bases of the leaves have spines. In recent years, it has been discovered that the use of lambda-cyhalothrin, a second-generation synthetic pyrethroid, is particularly efficient in lowering the number of pests on Earth.

e. Indigenous predators like *Santalus parallelus, Harpalus* sp., *Scarites* sp., *Pteropsophus occipitalis, Agrypnus* sp. nr. *Bifoveatus,* etc. suppress the immature stages of scarabaean. The entomopathogen, *Metarhizium anisopliae* produces epizootics within the natural population of scarabaeid beetle when the moisture levels of the breeding medium are 50% and also the temperature is 29oC and below (conditions ideal for mycosis) [38].

f. Application of *Metarhizium anisopliae* on the dead coconut logs is additionally proved effective in controlling the pest. The spores of the microbial organism are found viable till 9 months after preparation at room temperatures causing identical mortality to grub stages [39].

g. One of the most effective microbial control agents used to combat rhinoceros beetle infestation of coconut is the Baculovirus of *Oryctes*. The virus infection reduces the beetles' lifespan by 40% and completely eliminates their ability to reproduce. Wherever the virus was introduced into the pest's environment, an early epizootic wiped out populations of larvae and beetles, drastically reducing pest incidence and crop loss [40]. The most affordable, efficient, and simple way to spread the viral inoculum among the beetle population in its natural habitat is to release the infected insects [41].

h. Pheromone traps have a great deal of effectiveness capturing the floating population. Keeping rhinolure/oryctalurte sachets at a height of 10 feet per trap per 2 hectares inside the oil palm plantation using bucket vane traps. However, low humidity and high temperatures negate the pheromone's potential to attract bugs [42].

4.2.2 Cockchafer beetles (root grub): Apogonia/Adoretus *spp. (Scarabaeidae)*

Because grubs are visible throughout thc year, preferably in the first two to few months after planting, the incidence of adults is seen during the start of monsoon season (**Figure 9**).

4.2.2.1 Nature and symptoms of harm

The oil palm is harmed by adults as well as grubs. Young seedlings that are 1–2 months old have their roots killed by grubs, which causes seedling mortality. Defoliation is caused by adults killing the leaves. It is a problem in Karnataka's red soils and to a little extent in the entire state.

4.2.2.2 Management

The incidence of the grub stage is decreased by adding 20 g of phorate 10 g granules to each nursery bag, however the incidence of adults is effectively decreased by adding contact insecticides like quinalphos (0.05%).

Figure 9.
Cockchafer beetles (root grub).

4.3 Hemipteran pests

4.3.1 Spindle bug: Carvalhoia arecae *Miller (Miridae)*

It is primarily a significant pest of arecanut palms but also attained pest status on oil palms in Karnataka and Kerala states where arecanut is commercially grown. Spindle bug incidence and infestation were noticed very low in nursery seedlings and young plants. Throughout the year, infestation is observed, with June seeing the highest prevalence and, consequently, February seeing the lowest. When the palms got older, the percentage of infestation decreased, and 30 months after field planting, there was no sign of it [20]. The incidence is not reported aside from the above-mentioned states. The existence of low temperatures is also a critical factor for pest incidence (**Figure 10**).

4.3.1.1 Nature and symptoms of harm

As the nymphs and adults sip the sap from the fragile spear leaves, they are able to see the typical linear brown lesions. The spear leaves do not fully open when the infestation is bad. On the infected areas, necrotic patches form, which later turn brown and eventually dry up. Due to severe infestation, the leaves are torn apart by the necrotic patches, creating multiple holes in the leaves, which causes the palms to become stunted [23].

4.3.1.2 Management

Suppression of the bugs happens by an entomopathogenic fungus, *Aspergillus candidus* Link during the time of year, coinciding with the height period of its incidence [43]. An effective management technique is to apply phorate 10 g granules at 20 g each sachet inside the innermost two leaf axils [44]. With the appearance of new spindles, the phorate sachets are repeatedly relocated to the deepest leaf axils. The sachet lasts for roughly 8–10 months.

Figure 10.
Spindle bug on oil palm.

4.4 Homopteran pests

4.4.1 Leaf hopper, Proutista moesta *Westwood (Derbidae)*

On 10–14 month-old nursery plants in Kerala province, low leaf hopper incidence is seen in the months of September–October and once more in the months of January–February. Despite being harmless to seedlings, this has been shown to be a carrier of numerous viral and MLO diseases, most notably Spear rot (**Figure 11**) [45].

4.4.2 Aphids (Homoptera: Aphididae)

Schizaphis rotundiventris (Signoret) and *Mysteropneura setariae* (Thomas) infest the oil palm seedlings in state, particularly in area wherever the nurseries are encircled by sugarcane fields. *Astegopteryx rhaphides* (Van der Goot) has been found encrusting

Figure 11.
Leaf hopper, Proutista moesta.

the oil palm leaves in very little Andamans. The spears twist and warp due to the feeding on nursery plants. Jet-black mildew is developed because of honeydew melon secretion.

4.4.2.1 Management

Spraying of dimethoate zero.04% or monocrotophos zero.05% or insect powder zero.05% on the underside of the leaves is suggested for the management of aphids [23].

4.5 Coccoids (scales and mealy bugs)

Palmicultor palmarum (Ehrhorn) and *Nipaecoccus nipae* (Maskell) were observed on *Elaeis* in Ecuador. Two species of mealybugs, *Dysmicoccus brevipes* Cockerell and *Rhizoecus americanus* Hambleton, are found to cause damage to oil palms in Colombian nurseries. Some species live on the roots of *Elaeis*, such as *D. brevipes* Cockerell in Ecuador (**Figure 12**) [46].

In India, the spear leaves of oil palm seedlings in the nursery and field planted young oil palm seedlings are infested by *Pseudococus citricutus* Green, *Palmicultor* sp. and Margarodids, *Icerya aegyptiaca* (Douglas). *D. brevipes* infest the pre-anthesising male and female inflorescences and also unripe and ripe oil palm fruits [47–49]. Mealybugs on oil palm plants are migrants from other palmaeceae palms. Mealybugs are found in moist, warm climates. Mealy bugs are sporadic pests that are frequent in plantations, although they rarely cause outbreaks, which may be because of the work of natural enemies like coccinellid beetles whereas the primary indicators of endemic infestation are unsanitary circumstances and sanitation measures used in the gardens.

4.5.1 Nature and symptoms of damage

Coccids (soft scales) are noticed on the leaves of oil palms at all ages. Diaspids (armoured scales) are commonly found on the fruit bunches and leaves of oil palms. Sap from the tender spear leaves, inflorescence, and fruits is sucked by both nymphs and adult females. Attack by Diaspids results in the appearance of chlorotic spots on leaf tissues. These pests secrete a waxy cover, which hardens to form tough armour. The shape of the armour varies, being circular as in *Aspidiotus,* elongated/coma shaped/thread-like as in *Pinnaspis.* All the females live together and are protected by ants. Infestations of *Pseudococus citricutus* Green, Palrnicultor sp., *Margarodids, and Icerya aegyptiaca* (Douglas) have been found on the spear leaves of young oil palm seedlings that have been planted in the field and in nurseries. Both *Pseudococus* and *Palmicultor* species attack on spindle leaves of young plants resulting in the yellowing of unfolding leaves and stunted growth of the palm. Ring spots were not observed so far because continuous feeding causes a mottling appearance on leaves. Oil palm fruits of Fresh Fruit Bunches (FFB) are infested by *Dysmicoccus* spp. and they suck the mesocarp sap. These pests feed on plant sap and excrete honeydew which will attract ants and sooty mould development. The pest feeds only on ripe FFB and when the harvest is delayed, yield loss is more. It is also observed that the pest attack leads to the loosening of the fruits which leads to premature fruit drop.

Figure 12.
Scales and Mealy bugs on oil palm.

4.5.2 Management

a. Since ants frequently carry mealy bugs, the pest can be easily eliminated by suppressing ants and maintaining hygienic conditions in the garden. Endemic infestation is caused by unhygienic surroundings and sanitation procedures. Regular weeding and leaf cutting are found to keep pests from attacking the plantation.

b. Ladybird beetles are the most important predators of mealy bugs.

c. Mealybug infestations can be treated by spraying phosphamidon, dimethoate, or methyldemeton at concentrations of 0.025 or 0.05%, respectively. Malathion 0.1% can be sprayed to suppress scale insects.

4.6 Isopteran pests

4.6.1 Termites (Termitidae)

Seedlings kept in polybags, spear leaves, male and female inflorescences, and a field of newly planted seedlings have all been found to have termite infestations. Red soils make up the bulk of the soil types in locations where oil palms are grown, and termite incidence is also more common there. The breakdown of oil palm leftovers such clipped leaves, empty and decaying fruit bunches, and male inflorescences is observed to be accelerated by these good decomposers (**Figure 13**).

Figure 13.
Mound of Pericapritermes *on the palm roots, (b)* Hypotermes *mound beside oil palm tree, (c)* Pericapritermes *nest dug from the peat ground, (d)* Nasutitermes *sp. Nesting inside frond, (e)* Nasutitermes *sp. consuming the dead frond that laid on the ground and (f)* Odontotermes *devouring the decaying wood log.*

Two termite species, Pericapritermes sp. and Hypotermes sp., destroy the roots of seedlings kept in polybags in Karnataka, resulting in the seedlings' stunted growth. The infestation is most noticeable in oil palm fields with inadequate irrigation [20]. In the province's plantations, where the majority of the palm trees were exhibiting indications of clay sheathing over the stem position, this was frequently observed as severe. Due to the industry's rapid expansion, termite infestation in oil palm trees, particularly in peat soil, has become a serious issue in Malaysia. *Odontotermes* spp. are the most prevalent pest species in India's oil palm growing regions overall [32, 50, 51].

4.6.1.1 Nature and symptoms of injury

The pest was identified to be feeding on the trunk in addition to the opposite dried material, such as leaf butts, male inflorescence, dried/bunch rot, bunch failure, and infected FFBs. The infestation was first seen over the winter, and by the end of March or beginning of April, it had reached its peak. Though they are found feeding only on the dried and useless things and causing no death blow to the palms, however, it makes the palms seem ugly and indicates the poor maintenance of the orchards.

The earthen sheathings that are formed over the foraging areas are made from subsoil containing high amounts of potash and are beneficial in enhancing soil fertility [52–54]. By eating on the plant's collar section, which has distinctive clay wrapping on the stem portion, termites have been discovered to kill young nursery seedlings. Plants that are yielding and poorly managed nurseries are more vulnerable to termite attack. Due to termite occurrence in entirely abandoned plantations, adult producing palms are also discovered dead. Termite activity in irrigated oil palm plantations does not reduce yields, but it gives the plantation an unsightly appearance. In addition, the termite mounds on the plantation may develop into reptile nests, alarming the worker force.

4.6.1.2 Management

a. The use of entomopathogenic fungi, such as *Beauveria bassiana* and *Metarhizium anisopliae*, has shown considerable promise for the control of a variety of insect pests [55].

b. Chlorpyriphos 0.05% is typically advised for drenching [23].

4.7 Molluscan pests

Laevicaulis alte, a black slug, is a sporadic pest that feeds on oil palm nursery plants that are one day old. The pest is observed feeding on nursery plants that are put within the main bags and are still in their embryonic stages. It is observed travelling from the neighbouring remnants and debris of harvested crops, such as bananas. After the crop is removed, several bugs are discovered hiding beneath the banana stumps that are dumped. It occurs frequently during the season. It can be seen travelling during this time along with the water. They enter the nursery when it is already dark and feed on the newly planted sprouts. The most common methods used to control this pest include blocking pest entry sites within the greenhouse, applying salt pellets to raised bunds on all sides of the greenhouse, keeping the lights on at night inside the greenhouse, etc. (**Figure 14**) [56].

4.8 Vertebrate pests

4.8.1 Avian pests

Birds and rodents are the key pests of oil palm within the oil palm-growing countries of the planet. Both of them go after the mesocarp of Fresh Fruit Bunches (FFB) and cause direct losses in yield. Several species of birds cause extensive damage to oil palm fruits. Birds like crows, *Corvus* species; Mynah, *Acridotheres tristis*; Babbler, *Turdoides affinis*; Parrots, *Psitticula krameri* take advantage of the mesocarp of fruits causing an estimated fruit loss up to 2.8 t/ha/year. Of these, Indian mynah bird, Jungle crow, house crow, and parakeets cause significant fruit loss. The attack is observed throughout the year round and no seasonal variation in damage intensity is clear [57]. The great pied wagtail, coucal, pariah kite, white-headed babbler, and other birds occasionally eat oil palm fruits. Infestation is higher in ripe bunches (76%) compared to unripe bunches (5.6%). In comparison to Teneras (63%), Duras (84%) are more sensitive among the ripe bunches. However, Pisifera bunch damage is uncommon due to the low palm population and poor fruit setting brought on by sterility. In Madras,

Figure 14.
Black slug.

the districts of Trichy and Karur, where oil palm is grown in sparse areas, have significant incidences (>20–30%) of bird pests. When compared to crows, the incidence of myna was found to be higher (20–30%). Even when the bunches were covered with oil palm leaves, there was a high incidence of bird damage in the solitary oil palm gardens, with 100% damage. Since there is no alternative food source available to birds throughout the wet and summer seasons, they are more active in oil palm gardens during those times.

4.8.1.1 Nature and symptoms of injury

Birds deliberately cause harm by primarily eating mesocarp, leaving just fibres on the seeds. Birds may cause partial or total damage. Birds consume 40–50% of the weight of each fruit in fruit that is partially damaged. Weight loss of 68–73% may be seen in bunches with entire fruit destruction. All the fruits in many ripe fruit bunches are lost, resulting in a 100% loss in fruit weight. When fruit is first starting to ripen (130–150 days old), partial fruit damage is more prevalent, however complete fruit damage is found as fruit ripening progresses. Fruit loss in fully developed bunches of 160–180 days is incredibly high.

Bird damage to palm trees is worse in border areas (24.8%) compared to inside plantations (11.4%). Bird damage was estimated to cause an average loss of fruits per bunch of 2.3 kg in border palms and 1.3 kg in interior palms. A mean of 1.8 kg, or 4% of the mesocarp, was lost due to bird damage in each harvested bunch. In Malaysia, it is estimated that these bugs have caused a 30% loss. According to estimates, India loses two.8 tonnes of fresh fruit bundles (FFB) per hectare per year, equivalent to 420 kg of oil [58].

4.8.1.2 Management

a. A wire net with a 1.25 cm mesh (60 × 90 cm size), reed baskets, baskets made of plaited coconut leaves, or oil palm leaves should be used to cover ripe fruit bunches after 150 days of fruit set to prevent bird damage [47].

b. It is discovered to be efficient and affordable to cover the bunches with oil palm leaf tips and tie them with a piece of rope to keep them solid and impenetrable by the bird's beak.

c. It has been discovered that the easiest way to control the threat is to tie nylon fishnets measuring 9 by 1 metre between two palms. The best type of net to use to capture all birds has 5 sq. cm-sized holes. Nylon. A median of 5 nets per ha could provide the greatest benefit and are discovered to be ideal to rid the plantation of bird infestation. Within a month of being put into use, green and violet-coloured fishnets are easier to use and trap more birds, lowering the % infestation to zero [58].

d. The use of glue traps and sticky glue has not been demonstrated to be useful in reducing the incidence [56].

e. Tying the dead eagles within the periphery of the orchard to scare the birds entering the garden may be a commonly seen practice that's unique. However, it's not effective.

4.8.2 Mammalian pests

Rat (*Ratus rattus* wroughtoni), House rat (*Rattus rattus* rufescens) Lesser bandicoot (*Bandicota bengalensis*), Larger bandicoot (*Bandicota indica*), Indian gerbil (*Tatera indica* cuvieri), Western Ghat squirrel (*Funambulus tristriatus*) and Procupines (*Hystrix indica*) attack oil palm at various stages of its development.

4.8.2.1 Nature and symptoms of injury

Burrowing rat, *T. indica* (Hardwicke) was found attacking the young oil palm plants by migrating from the adjacent maize fields further because the forest plants. They burrow all the way down to the bole region by making cavities to feed the cabbage tissue leading to the wilting of leaves and mortality of the palms. The immature fruit bunches that were between 2 and 3 months old were the principal food sources for the roof rat, *R. rattus* Linn. They were discovered drawn, taking use of the semi-solid apical mesocarp and kernel region of the fruit. Because the fruits were only partially chopped, the symptoms of an attack are visible. Rats consume both ripe and unripe bunches of fruit as well as the exposed pericarp of ripe and unripe fruits in mature palm trees [32]. Rodents use their incisors to attack the pericarp, creating distinctive gnawing imprints on fruits. Rats consume the grub and pupae of pollinating weevils while destroying the spikelets of the male inflorescences. Newly planted seedlings are dug up by a boar (*Sus scrofa*), who then eats them. If they are available, they also consume the fruits from the tree's bunches.

4.8.2.2 Management

a. By erecting barriers made of 1.25 cm mesh (Chickenwire mesh) collars around the base of young plants, damage can be avoided. To stop the rats from going inside or beneath the bottom, they must be tied tightly around the palm and all the way down.

b. As part of an integrated strategy, traps such as iron live traps, death fall traps, bow traps, etc. are also utilised to lessen rodent damage to oil palms.

c. Zinc phosphide and bromadiolone baiting are proven to be efficient against the rat threat. Comparing the effectiveness of zinc phosphide baiting with newspaper without hand protection, it was shown to be 33% more feasible to use banana leaves as packages.

d. A local method of preventing pigs from entering nurseries and young oil palm crops has been created. The plantation border is delineated by two lines of 20 cm-high, parallel-to-the-bottom 18-gauge G.I. wire fencing that is supported by poles and held in place by guide hooks. Depending on the land's topography, the poles are spaced anywhere between 3 and 10 m apart. With the aid of four poles, two crushing slabs, two oval plays, and a cracker, junction boxes can be constructed. Depending on the geographical limits, roads, etc., this might be spaced anywhere from 5 to 15 m apart. The aid of a crushing slab suspended from a third play kept on the primary two plays is used to join the two fence lines that arrive at the junction boxes from different sides onto the oval plays, pull them closer, and hold them in place. Under this crushing slab, crackers are maintained. When the animal strikes the fence, it will force the initial play to fall apart, causing the cracker to fall into the second crushing slab that is kept directly underneath and burst. The strategy has been found very effective in scaring away the animals [23, 59].

4.8.2.3 Wild boar, Sus scrofa

Wild boar is reported as a very important mammal causing heavy damage to the nursery in Andhra Pradesh, Karnataka, and Kerala states of India. The damage is seen mostly on the boll region of 18–24 months old seedlings. They are available in groups during the dusk period and go after the seedlings. The damage is found more because of their disturbance compared to their eating. Boar scaring devices like putting electric fencing and other smoking devices are found futile (**Figure 15**).

DOI: http://dx.doi.org/10.5772/intechopen.108580

Figure 15.
Wild boar Sus scrofa *in oil palm garden.*

4.8.2.4 Black rat, Rattus rattus *Wroughtoni.*

Rat incidence on oil palm seedlings is recorded in all the nurseries. It is more serious in poorly managed nurseries. They're found feeding on the kernel portion of the nuts causing mortality to the seedlings. Incidence is so severe when the spreading of primary seedlings is not done even after 6 months and where the soil is drained therefore the roots are exposed due to poor irrigation practices. In Mizoram, Boi (bamboo rat *Cannomys badius*) could be a common pest feeding on the roots of the newly planted oil palms (**Figure 16**).

Figure 16.
Black rat furrowing in oil palm garden.

5. Integrated pest management (IPM) practices

The following are the most significant IPM additives, listed in increasing order of complexity:

5.1 Cultural practices

To eliminate pests or stop them from causing financial harm is one way cultural pest management systems incorporate routine farm tasks. Here is a list of the numerous cultural traditions.

- Methods used to get nursery or main fields free of pest infestation include removing plant debris, pruning bunds, treating soil, and deep midsummer ploughing (which kills a number of pests).
- Vitamin deficiency in the soil is tested to determine which fertilisers should be used.
- Choosing clean, authorised seeds and treating them with fungicides or bio-insecticides prior to sowing to control seed-borne disease.
- Proper plant spacing, which increases plant health and reduces pest risk.
- It is important to encourage the use of biofertilizers, FYM, and effective fertilisers.
- Appropriate water management since excessive wetness in the soil over an extended period of time encourages the growth of pests, particularly those that spread diseases through the soil.
- Effective weed control as it is a well-known undisputed fact that almost all weeds not only compete with crops for micronutrients but also house a variety of pests.
- Placing area yellow pan sticky traps for aphids and white flies a few inches above the ground.
- Synchronised sowing- Here, a network strategy is required to sow the plant simultaneously over a very big area so that pests will not be able to acquire distinctively staged vegetation suitable for increasing their population. If there are too many pests, the procedure is frequently correctly carried out throughout the entire area.
- Vegetation that is enticingly growing along field edges. It goes without saying that a certain pest species favours some plants over others, and these plants are known to attract that insect. Pest populations rise as a result of the vegetation that is grown around the fields' edges; these populations can be reduced either by employing pesticides or by promoting the growth of their natural enemies for herbal management.
- Intercropping or several crops whenever possible. Every pest species does not appear to be attracted to any particular vegetation, and since desirable vegetation serves as repellents to keep pest species away from it, the incidence of pests is reduced.
- Harvesting as close to the stage of the floor. This is because insect pests and diseases with favourable developmental stages remain on plant components,

serving as the primary inoculum for the following crop season. Therefore, cutting down on pests in the following season by picking plants at the floor stage.

- To protect nursery plants from soil-borne diseases, nursery plants are sprayed with copper fungicide or biopesticide solutions before planting.
- Throw away crowded, dead, damaged, or diseased branches and destroy them when pruning fruit trees. Avoid piling them inside orchards because this could serve as a source of pest infestation.
- To shield plants from pest and disease attacks, apply Bordeaux paste or paint to big pruning wounds.
- •Bee hives and floral arrangements designed to attract pollinators promote increased pollination and the subsequent fruit set.
- The choice of high-yielding pest resistant/tolerant varieties.

5.2 Mechanical practices

It is feasible to remove and destroy hundreds of insect pests' eggs, larvae, pupae, and adults as well as disease-related components of plant life from any location.

- Putting hundreds of parasitized eggs within bamboo cages with hen perchers installed inside the sphere to preserve natural enemies and, whenever feasible, keep pest species away.
- The use of light traps and the eradication of captured insects.
- Installing the necessary hen scarer inside the sphere and adding hen perches inside the sphere to allow birds to perch there while navigating bugs and their juvenile stages, such as eggs, larvae, and pupae.
- The use of pheromones to create new areas and stop mating and pheromone traps to monitor and control the population of pests by mass capturing using.

5.3 Regulatory practices

In this procedure, governmental regulations are put into effect that prevent seeds and plant materials that have been infected from entering the country or moving from one region to another. These are referred to as quarantine techniques and come in two flavours: domestic and international.

5.4 Biological practices

The most important aspect of IPM is biological control of diseases and insect pests through biological methods. Biocontrol, in a more general meaning, is the use of living things to control other living things (pests). In other words, the deliberate use of parasitoids, predators, and diseases to control pest populations at a level below those resulting in economic loss, either by introducing a new bioagent into the environment of pests or by increasing the effectiveness of those already present in the field.

5.4.1 Parasitoids

These are the organisms that deposit their eggs in or on their hosts' bodies and then finish their life cycles there, killing their hosts in the process. A parasitoid can also come in a variety of forms depending on where it is in the host's development or how far along it is in its life cycle. As examples, consider *Apanteles*, *Bracon*, *Chelonus*, *Brachemeria*, and different *Trichogramma* species, among others.

5.4.2 Predators

These are free-living organisms that feed on the other living things. Examples include several spider species, dragonfly and damsel species, ladybird beetles, *Chrysopa* species, and birds, among others.

5.4.3 Bio-pesticides

These are microorganisms that attack and infect their hosts, resulting in diseases that kill the hosts. Pathogens can be divided into three primary groups: bacteria, viruses, and fungi. Some nematodes can also transmit diseases to pest insects. Species of *Hirsutella*, *Beauveria*, *Nomuria*, and *Metarhizium* are important examples of fungi because they are known to infest and kill a lot of insects in fields (up to 90%). The nuclear polyhedrosis virus (NPV) and granulosis viruses are the two most significant instances of viruses. There have been numerous reports of an outbreak of viruses in armyworms, cutworms, leaf folders, hairy caterpillars, and plant hoppers. *Bacillus thuringiensis* (Bt) and *B. papillae* are two typical examples of bacteria.

Sometimes, with the use of liquid or powdered formulations that can be sprayed like conventional chemical pesticides, pest diseases can be mass-produced in laboratories at a cost. Bio-pesticides are the name given to these mixtures. The several types of biocontrol techniques are categorised as follows:

Introduction: A replacement species of bio-agent is dispersed into the area during this phase in order to establish itself against its host. This is frequently done only after careful laboratory analysis and field tests to determine its efficacy.

Augmentation: By releasing identical species bio-agents from the field or from a lab in sufficient numbers to suppress the pest population in the area, the population of natural enemies already present in the area is boosted throughout this process.

Conservation: This is frequently the most crucial element of biological management and is crucial in the control of pests. Natural adversaries that exist in nature are protected from being killed during this process. Below are the numerous precautions that must be taken to protect against natural adversaries.

- Collecting parasitized egg masses and putting them in bamboo cages with bird perches to let parasitoids develop and keep pest larvae at bay.

- Using field days, radio shows, and television to teach farmers how to tell the difference between pests and defenders in order to prevent spraying defenders.

- Following observation of the pest defender ratio, chemical spray should be used as a last option as well.
- It is best to avoid using broad-spectrum pesticides. Only selective and comparatively eco-friendly (REF) pesticides should be used, where appropriate. Pesticides should always be used in spot or strip treatments. Use insecticides according to the recommended dose and concentration.
- Changing planting and harvesting times to prevent the insect attack's peak period.
- Planting trap crops on the edges of main fields before a specific crop is sown in order to trap pests and foster the growth of natural enemies.
- Intercropping and crop rotation both aid in the conservation of defenders.

5.5 Chemical practices

Chemical pesticides are only used as a last resort if all other efforts have failed to reduce the insect population below the point of economic loss. Due to the complexity of insect problems, pesticides would still be necessary for crop protection despite substantial advancements in pest control research. Therefore, to limit both the cost and issues they create, pesticide use should be need-based, judicious, and supported by pest surveillance. When employing chemicals to control an area, we must have a complete understanding of what to spray, when to spray, where to spray, and how to spray.

- The pest defender ratio must be kept in mind.
- If the pest is only present in strips or isolated patches, the entire field should not be sprayed; instead, choose relatively safer pesticides, such as neem-based and biopesticides.

Due of the distinct way that vegetables and fruits are consumed by people, IPM approaches are especially pertinent to these crops. For the recommended crops, only pesticides that have been certified by the CIB&RC should be used. After the primary pesticide's waiting period is through, farmers should not use any additional pesticides, and the crops should be harvested. Applying pest management techniques to field crops must be done with the utmost care and caution.

6. Conclusion

The sustainability of oil palm cultivation is the need of the hour for both farmers as well as processors and finally the enrichment of the economy. To minimise losses, it is crucial to control the insect population below economic threshold levels. In order to achieve this, integrated management techniques that improve the sustainability of the oil palm industry as a whole must be established employing the most recent low-cost technologies.

Acknowledgements

My due acknowledgments are to the Management, Koneru Lakshmaiah Education Foundation, Vaddeswaram, Guntur, Andhra Pradesh-522302, India for their immense support and encouragement in promoting research.

Conflict of interest

"The authors declare no conflict of interest."

Author details

Rajasekhar Pinnamaneni[1]* and Kalidas Potineni[2]

1 Department of Biotechnology, Koneru Lakshmaiah Education Foundation, Vaddeswaram, Andhra Pradesh, India

2 ICAR-Indian Institute of Oil palm Research, Andhra Pradesh, India

*Address all correspondence to: pinnamaneniraj@yahoo.com

References

[1] Kamarudin N, Arshad O. Potentials of using the pheromone trap for monitoring and controlling the bagworm, Metisa plana Wlk (Lepidoptera: Psychidae) on young oil palm in a smallholder plantation. Journal of Asia-Pacific Entomology. 2006;**9**(3): 281-285. DOI: 10.1016/S1226-8615(08) 60304-0

[2] Cheong YL, Sajap AS, Hafidzi MN, Omar D, Abood F. Outbreaks of bagworms and their natural enemies in an oil palm, Elaeis guineensis, Plantation at Hutan Melintang, Perak Malaysia. Journal of Entomology. 2010; **7**(3):141-151. DOI: 10.3923/ je.2010.141.151

[3] Brader L. Integrated pest control in the developing world. Annual Review of Entomology. 1979;**24**(1):225-254. DOI: 10.1146/annurev.en.24.010179. 001301

[4] Wood BJ. Pest control in Malaysia's perennial crops: A half century perspective tracking the pathway to integrated pest management. Integrated Pest Management Reviews. 2002;**7**(3): 173-190. DOI: 10.1023/B: IPMR.0000027501.91697.49

[5] Hamid NH, Abidin Z, Rizuan CK, Suhaidi H. Control Measures and Integrated Approach for Major Pests of Oil Palm in FELDA. MPOB Palm Oil Congress (PIPOC). 2013. pp. 1-21

[6] Syed RA. Insect pollination of oil palm: Feasibility of introducing Elaeidobius spp. into Malaysia. In: Chew P, editor. The Oil Palm in the Eighties. A Report of the Proceedings of the International Conference on Oil Palm in Agriculture in the Eighties, Kuala Lumpur. 1981. p. I

[7] Greathead DJ. The multi-million dollar weevil that pollinates oil palms. Antenna. 1983;**7**(3):105-107

[8] Ponnamma KN, Dhileepan K, Sasidharan VG. Record of the pollinating weevil Elaeidobius kamerunicus (Faust) (Coleoptera: Curculionidae) in oil palm plantations of Kerala. Current Science India. 1986;**55**(19): 992-993

[9] Syed RA. Studies on oil palm pollination by insects. Bulletin of Entomological Research. 1979;**69**(2): 213-224. DOI: 10.1017/ S0007485300017673

[10] Pushparajah E, Chew PS. The Oil Palm in Agriculture in the Eighties (in Two Volumes). Incorporated Society of Planters: Kuala Lumpur; 1982

[11] Yue J, Yan Z, Bai C, Chen Z, Lin W, Jiao F. Pollination activity of Elaeidobius kamerunicus (Coleoptera: Curculionoidea) on oil palm on Hainan Island. Entomologiste. 2015;**98**(2): 499-505. DOI: 10.1653/024.098.0217

[12] Zulkefli MHH, Jamian S, Adam NA, Jalinas J, Mohamad SA, Mohd Masri MM. Beyond four decades of Elaeidobius kamerunicus Faust (Coleoptera: Curculionidae) in the Malaysian oil palm industry: A review. Journal of Tropical Ecology. 2020; **36**(6):282-292. DOI: 10.1017/ S026646742000022X

[13] Mat Daud SNS, Abd GI. Population density of oil palm pollinator weevil Elaeidobius kamerunicus based on seasonal effect and age of oil palm. AIP Conference Proceedings. 2016;**1784**:060051. DOI: 10.1063/1.4966889

[14] Greathead DJ, Greathead AH. Biological control of insect pests by insect parasitoids and predators: The BIOCAT database. Biocontrol News and Information. 1992;**13**(4):61N-68N. DOI: 10.1079/cabireviews/19921166435

[15] Kang SM, Karim Z, Heong KL, Lee BS, Lim TM, Teoh CH et al. Quarantine aspects of the introduction into Malaysia of an oil palm insect pollinator. In: Proceedings of the International Conference on Plant Protection in the Tropics. Kuala Lumpur, Malaysia; 1-4 March 1982. pp. 615-626

[16] Poinar GO, Jackson TA, Bell NL, Wahid MB. Elaeolenchus parthenonema n. g., n. sp. Systematic Parasitology. 2002;**52**(3):219-225. DOI: 10.1023/a:1015741820235

[17] Ahmad MN, Ali SRA, Masri MMM, Wahid MB. Effect of Bt products, Lepcon-1, Bafog-1 (S) and Ecobac-1 (EC), against the oil palm pollinating weevil, Elaeidobius kamerunicus, and beneficial insects associated with Cassia cobanensis. Journal of Oil Palm Research. 2012;**24**:1442-1447

[18] Kalidas P, Rajasekhar P, Lalitha SVL. Impact of pesticides on the pollinating weevils of oil palm. Journal of Plantation Crops. 2008;**36**(3):460-462

[19] Wood BJ. Pests of Oil Palms in Malaysia and Their Control. Kuala Lumpur, Malaysia: The Incorporated Society of Planters; 1968. p. 222

[20] Dhileepan K. Insect Pests of Oil Palm (Elaeis Guineensis) in India. Vol. 68. Kuala Lumpur: The Planter; 1992 p. 183-91

[21] Syed RA, Saleh HA. Integrated Pest management of bagworms in oil palm plantations of PTPP London Sumatra, Indonesia TBK (with particular reference to Mahasena corbetti Tams) in north Sumatra. In: Proceedings of the 1998 International Oil Palm Conference. Bali, Indonesia: Nusa Dua; 1998. p. 7

[22] Mariau D. Knowledge of oil palm pests and population management. In: Proceedings of the 1999 PORIM International Palm Oil Congress (Agriculture). Kuala Lumpur, Malaysia; 1999. pp. 129-138

[23] Nair CPR, Daniel M. Pests. In: KVA B, Nair MK, Premkumar T, editors. The Arecanut Palm, A Monograph. Central Plantation Crops Re-search Institute: Kasaragod, India; 1982

[24] Kalidas P. Pest problems of oil palm and management strategies for sustainability. Agrotechnology. 2012;**S11**: 001. DOI: 10.4172/2168-9881.S11-001

[25] Ricardo ST, Rafel CR, Marcelo TT, Evaldo FV, Walkymario DPL, Jose CZFE. Brachymeria spp. (Hymenoptera: Chalcididae) parasitizing pupae of Hersperidae and Nymphalidae (Lepidopera) pests of oil palm in the Brazilian Amazonian region. Florida Entomologist. 2012;**95**(3):788-789

[26] Kalidas P, Rethinam P. Incidence of leaf web formers on oil palm. Programme and Abstracts, National Seminar on Oil Palm Research and Development in 21st Century. Pedavegi: NRC for Oil Palm; 1998. p. 31

[27] Kalidas P. Susceptibility of oil palm (Tenera hybrid) planting material for rhinoceros beetle, Oryctes rhinoceros L. Journal of Plantation Crops. 2004; **32**(Suppl):385-387

[28] Shashank PR, Saravanan L, Kalidas P, Phanikumar T, Ramamurthy VV, Chandra Bose NS. A new species of the genus Acria Stephens,

1834 (Lepidoptera: Depressariidae: Acriinae) from India. Zootaxa. 2015; **3957**(2):226-230. DOI: 10.11646/ zootaxa.3957.2.6

[29] Saravanan L, Kalidas P, Phani KT. Investigations on oil palm leaf web worm, Acria sp.: An emerging serious pest of oil palm. In: Admin S, editor. Global Conference on Horticulture for Food, Nutrition and Livelihood Options". 28-31st. Bhubaneswar, Orissa; 2012. pp. 233-234

[30] Jacob SA, Kochu BM. Sesamia inferens, a new pest of oil palm seedlings. The planter, Kuala Lumpur. 1995;**71**(831):265-266

[31] Dhileepan K. Insects associated with oil palm (Elaeis guineensis) in India. FAO Plant Prothology Bull. 1991;**39**: 94-97

[32] Kalidas P, Ramprasad KV, Rammohan K. Pest status in irrigated oil palm orchards of coastal areas of India. Journal of Indian Society for Coastal Agricultural Research. 2002;**20**(1):41-50

[33] Kalidas P, Venkateswara Rao C, Ali N, Kochu BM. New pest incidence on oil palm seedlings in India- A study of black slug (Laevicaulus alte). The Planter Kuala Lumpur. 2006;**82**(960): 181-186

[34] Kalidas P. Strategies on pest management in oil palm. In: Dhawan AK, Singh B, Singh R, Bhuller MB, editors. Recent Trends in Integrated Pest Management. Indian Society for the Advancement of Insect Science; 2011. pp. 177-185

[35] Dhileepan K. Incidence and intensity of rhinoceros beetle infestation in the oil palm plantations in India. Journal Plantation of Crops. 1988;**16**: 126-129

[36] Ponnamma KN, Lalitha N, Sajeeb KA. Oil palm mesocarp waste a potential breeding me-dium for rhinoceros beetle, Oryctes rhinoceros L. International Journal of Oil Palm Research. 2001;**2**(1):37-40

[37] CPCRI. Annual Report for 1992–93. Central plantation Crops Research Institute. Kasaragod: India; 1993

[38] Sundarababu PC, Balasubramanian M, Jayaraj S. Studies on the Pathogenicity of Metarhizium anisopliae (metschnikoff) Sorokin var. Major Tulloch on Oryctes rhinoceros (L.). Vol. 1. Communication Centre, Directorate of Extension Education. Tamil Nadu Agricultural University. 1993. pp. 29-32

[39] Kalidas P. Stress management of insect pests on oil palm, Elaeis guineensis Jacq. Journal of Oilseeds Research. 2004; **21**(1):220-223

[40] Pillai GB, Sathiamma B, Danger TK. Integrated control of rhinoceros beetle. In: Nair MK, Khan HH, Gopalasundaram P, Rao EVVB, editors. Advances in Coconut Research and Development. Kasaragod: Central Plantation Crops Research Institute; 1993. pp. 58-65

[41] Dhileepan K. Impact of release of Baculovirus oryctes into a population of Oryctes rhinoceros in an oil palm plantation in India. The Planter. 1994;**70**: 255-266

[42] Alidas P. Effect of abiotic factors on the efficiency of rhinoceros beetle pheromone oryctalure in the oil palm growing areas of Andhra Pradesh. The Planter. 2004;**80**(935):103-115

[43] Dhileepan K, Nair RR, Leena S. Aspergillus candidus Link, as an entomopathogen of spindle bug,

Carvalhoia arecae M & C (Miriidae; Heteroptera). The planter. Kuala Lumpur. 1990;**66**:519-521

[44] Jacob SA. Distribution of the spindle bug of arecanut, Carvalhoia arecae Miller and China in Kerala, its bio-ecology, suspected role as a vector of yellow leaf disease and control. Series/Report No: RNT VIII (131). Palode, Trivendrum: Central Plantation Crops Research Institute; 1990

[45] Kochu BM. Spear rot of oil palm (Elaeis guineensis Jacq.) in India. Journal Plantation of Crops. 1989;**16**(Suppl): 281-286

[46] Mariau D. The Fauna of Oil Palm and Coconut – Insect and Mite Pests and Their Natural Enemies. France: CIRAD; 2001. p. 213

[47] Dhileepan K, Jacob SA. Pests. In: Oil Palm Prod Technol. Palode: CPCRI, RC; 1996. pp. 49-58

[48] Ponnamma KN. Coccoids associated with oil palm in India – a review. The Planter. 1999;**75**(882):445-451

[49] Kalidas P. Oil palm. In: Mani M, Shivaraju C, editors. Mealybugs and Their Management in Agricultural and Horticultural Crops. India: Springer; 2016. pp. 569-71

[50] Kalidas P, Lavanya P. Termite management of in oil palm ecosystem using microbial organisms. Indian Journal Soil Biology Ecology. 2014;**35** (1&2):257-265

[51] Kalidas P. Studies on termites, *Odontotermes* spp. with special reference to their role in the fertility of soil. Ph.D thesis. Bangalore, India: University of Agricultural Sciences; 1986. p. 123

[52] Kalidas P, Veeresh GK. Plant growth in mound soils of Odontotermes species. Indian Journal of Agricultural Sciences. 1989;**59**(1):8-10

[53] Kalidas P, Veeresh GK. Effect of termite foraging on soil fertility. In: Social Insects and the Environment. Proceedings of the 11th International Congress of International Union of the Study of the Social Insects (IUSSI), 5-11th August, 1990. Bangalore I: Oxford & IBH. Publications; 1990. pp. 608-609

[54] Inglis GD, Goettel MS, Butt TM, Strasser H. Use of Hyphomycetous fungi for managing insect pests. In: Butt TM, Jachson C, Magan N, editors. Fungi as Biocontrol Agents: Progress, Problems and Potential. Wallingford, UK: CABI Publishing; 2001. pp. 23-69

[55] Kalidas P. Avian pest menace in oil palm and the impact of novel technologies on its management. Journal Plantation of Crops. 2006;**34**:172-178

[56] Dhileepan K. Investigations on avian pests of oil palm, Elaeis guineensis Jacq in India. Tropical Pest Management. 1989;**35**(3):273-277. DOI: 10.1080/09670878909371379

[57] Dhileepan K. Trials on the protection of oil palm fruit bunch from bird damage in India. The Planter. 1990;**66**:171-177

[58] Kalidas P, Vasudevarao V. New Technology for the Management of Bird Menace in Oil Palm. Pedavegi: National Seminar on Research and development of Oil Palm in India, NRC for Oil Palm; 2005. p. 173

[59] Jacob SA. A simple device for scaring away wild boar (Sus scrofa) in newly planted oil palm fields. The Planter. 1993;**69**(811):475-477